CULTURES OF THE WORLD

SPAIN

Elizabeth Kohen

MARSHALL CAVENDISH
New York • London • Sydney

Reference edition reprinted 2000 by
Marshall Cavendish Corporation
99 White Plains Road
Tarrytown
New York 10591

© Times Media Private Limited 1995, 1992

Originated and designed by
Times Books International, an imprint of
Times Media Private Limited, a member of the
Times Publishing Group

Printed in Malaysia

Library of Congress Cataloging-in-Publication Data:
Kohen, Elizabeth Robin, 1960–
    Spain / Elizabeth Robin Kohen.—Reference ed.
      p. cm.—(Cultures Of The World)
    Includes bibliographical references and index.
    Summary: Introduces the geography, history, economy,
    culture, and people of Spain.
    ISBN 1-85435-451-5
    1. Spain—Juvenile literature. [1. Spain.]
I. Title. II. Series.
DP17.K6 1992
946—dc20   91–40373
                          CIP
                          AC

INTRODUCTION

A CULTURAL CROSSROADS of European and Moorish influences, Spain is rich in beauty and contrasts. From rugged mountain ranges to soft-sand beaches, from dazzling white cities to Gothic cathedrals and mosques, from colorful religious festivals to dramatic bullfights, Spain beguiles the senses.

One of the most ancient countries in Europe, Spain has survived numerous conquerors and conquests, religious fervor, and expansionism. It has seen power and glory during the days of the Catholic Kings and then watched it all decline. What followed were unstable rule, civil war, right-wing fanaticism, and days of darkness and obscurity. But now, Spain is poised on the brink of economic stability and renewed cultural splendor.

This book, part of the series *Cultures of the World,* will take a look at this remarkable country, its peoples, and their lifestyle.

CONTENTS

A boy sits on the step of a medieval building in the Gothic quarter, Barcelona.

CONTENTS

Spanish women dressed in traditional costumes at a harvest fiesta in Jerez, southern Spain.

GEOGRAPHY

SPAIN, EUROPE'S third largest nation, is more than twice the size of Oregon. It occupies most of the Iberian peninsula at the western edge of the continent and has an area of 195,988 square miles (507,609 sq. km), including the Balearic and Canary Islands. Spanish territory comprises the mainland (which contains about 98% of the national territory), the Balearic Islands in the Mediterranean Sea, the Canary Islands off the west coast of Africa, and the cities of Ceuta and Melilla—Spanish free ports facing Andalusia on the northern African coast in Morocco. Mainland Spain borders France and Andorra to the north, Gibraltar to the south, and Portugal to the west. The entire east coast of Spain borders the Mediterranean Sea.

Opposite: **Costa Brava, Spain's "wild coast" along the Mediterranean, is characterized by its jutting rocks and rugged profile.**

Below: **Country villages nestle in the plains of Alicante, surrounded by rolling hills.**

One of Spain's most striking geographical features is its extensive mountain ranges in the north and south of the country, and on its offshore islands. The second highest country in Europe, after Switzerland, Spain has an average elevation of 2,165 feet (660 m), with one-quarter of its surface area rising to 3,280 feet (999 m) above sea level. Another remarkable feature is the Meseta, a plateau found in the center of the country. Making up almost half of the Spanish mainland, it is the largest plateau of its kind in Europe. Spain also boasts a coastline some 2,600 miles (4,183 km) long. This variation in topography makes for an interesting variety of climate and natural resources.

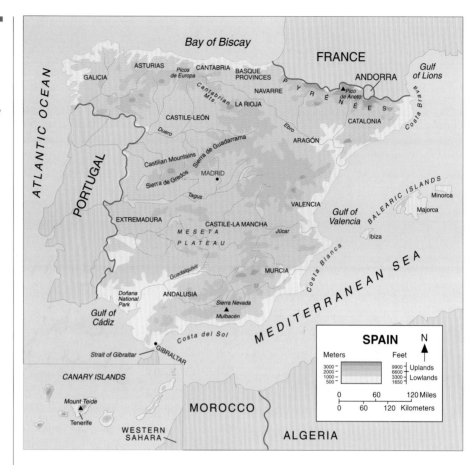

MAINLAND REGIONS

The Spanish mainland can be broadly divided into five distinct regions.

GREEN SPAIN Located in the north and northwest, Green Spain comprises the regions of Galicia, Asturias, Cantabria, and the Basque provinces. Green Spain is aptly named, for it has a wet, evergreen climate typical of northwestern European countries, such as England. Moss covers rock formations and ancient ruins along the mostly rural landscape. The region also has its share of coastline, which is mostly rugged, with steep cliffs and great rocky inlets called *rias* ("REE-uhs").

The Cantabrian Mountains, which extend roughly 300 miles (483 km) along northern and northwestern Spain and rise to 8,794 feet (2,679 m) at the highest point, have helped to create a barrier between this region of Spain and the rest of the country. The mountain range features some of the country's wildest landscapes, while the Basque countryside, occupying the eastern part of the Cantabrian Mountains, is an unusual mixture of idyllic mountain villages and smoky industries.

INLAND SPAIN Made up of La Rioja, Castile-León, Castile-La Mancha, Extremadura, and Madrid, this region is characterized by its austere elevated plateaus and arid climate. Madrid, with a population of 4.5 million, has been Spain's capital since the 16th century.

Surrounding Madrid is a variety of scenery and terrain. The Sierras of Guadarrama and Gredos to the north of Madrid provide perfect winter playgrounds, while south of Madrid, the land turns harsh and sunbaked. La Rioja, a small region of farmland to the north of Madrid, is known for its extensive vineyards. The huge region of Castile, which surrounds Madrid, includes the ancient kingdoms of Castile and León and the region of La Mancha. The region is located on a vast plateau, the Meseta, which has a harsh, melancholy appearance. A stony landscape is one of the dominant features of the Castilian countryside; the fields surrounding the cities of Ávila and Segovia are littered with boulders. The soil is poor here, as it also is in Extremadura, a wild remote region that is recognized as the pure essence of Spain because much of Extremadura has resisted modernization.

Much of the Castilian countryside is lightly populated. Here, isolated villages and medieval ruins dot the vast and desolate sun-scorched plains.

The Mediterranean coast is well populated. The coastal cities, towns, and villages are known for their abundance of seafood.

THE PYRÉNÉES Navarre and Aragón, both former medieval kingdoms, are regions whose northern tips abut the Pyrénées Mountains. The rugged mountain chain extends for 260 miles (418 km) between the Bay of Biscay and the Mediterranean Sea and rises to 11,168 feet (3,403 m) at Pico de Aneto, the highest point. The Pyrénées include three main ranges: the Catalan Pyrénées, the Central Pyrénées in Aragón, and the Pyrénées of Navarre. Throughout the mountainous region, there are upper meadows, pasture land, glacial lakes, and streams. At the foot of the mountains lie a series of valleys that turn to fertile orchards and vineyards at the Ebro River basin.

MEDITERRANEAN SPAIN This includes the regions of Catalonia, Valencia, and Murcia. The region of Catalonia is geographically the most diverse. In the shadow of the northeastern portion of the Pyrénées, Catalonia's landscape changes from cold valleys to fertile *huertas* ("WEHR-tahs"), coastal or irrigated plains rich with citrus orchards. Barcelona, the capital of Catalonia, has a population of about four million.

Valencia, too, has many orchards, and palm and fig trees. Murcia is the smallest and driest part of the Mediterranean region. Its hills, dotted with fertile *huertas* moistened by irrigated waters, yield excellent produce.

SOUTHERN SPAIN With a mild climate year-round in most of the region, Andalusia is one of the top tourist spots in Spain. Nowhere else is the legacy of 750 years of Moorish occupation so alive.

The natural landscape of this region varies from east to west. In the east lie the snowcapped majestic heights of the Sierra Nevada, whose peak Mulhacén is the highest point on the mainland, rising to 11,411 feet (3,477 m). High on these slopes are numerous little mountain villages. The fertile plains of Granada, lying at the foot of the Sierra Nevada, brim with tobacco fields and poplar groves. The dry desert landscape of the coastal city of Almería contrasts with the fertile soils and plains of cities only miles away.

The Guadalquivir River, known to the Arabs as the "great river," crosses the whole region, flowing 374 miles (602 km) west to the Atlantic Ocean. In its course westward, it crosses the olive groves of Jaén and the fruit and nut orchards of Córdoba. The fertile flat pastures, vineyards, and mostly white sand beaches of western Andalusia contrast with the mountain provinces in the east. Here, along the banks of the Guadalquivir, the land is lined with cotton and rice fields, citrus groves, and bull ranches that breed *toros bravos* ("TOH-rohs BRAH-bos"), bulls that fight in the ring.

Bright white-washed houses are typical of Seville.

Seville is the capital of Andalusia and the third largest city in Spain, with a population of about 683,000. The ancient city of Cádiz is in Andalusia. Located on a narrow strip of land, surrounded by the Atlantic Ocean, Cádiz claims to be the oldest continuously inhabited city in the Western world.

Snowcapped most of the year, Mount Teide on the island of Tenerife is composed of numerous small, active craters and a large, dormant one, 200 feet (61 m) in diameter.

THE CANARY AND BALEARIC ISLANDS

The Canary Islands are an archipelago of seven islands located in the Atlantic near the Tropic of Cancer and opposite the African coast, 650 miles (1,046 km) from the Spanish mainland. The islands are of volcanic origin, with varied geological formations and abundant tropical vegetation. On the island of Tenerife, Mount Teide, the highest point in all of Spain, rises to 12,195 feet (3,715 m). The Canaries also have desert-like areas rich in minerals, black lava cliffs, a warm, dry climate year-round, and rare botanical species.

The Balearic Islands lie 50 to 150 miles (80 to 241 km) from eastern Spain's Mediterranean coast, a position that made the islands an important strategic post for invaders and settlers throughout Spain's history. There are three main islands, each with a distinctive character. Majorca, mountainous on its northwestern side, hilly on the southeast, and flat and full of olive and almond groves elsewhere, is the largest island of the group (five times the size of either Minorca or Ibiza) and the site of Palma, the Balearic capital. Ibiza is world-renowned as a popular vacation spot. Megalithic monuments left over from pre-Roman cultures dot the landscapes of Minorca and Majorca.

CLIMATE

Spain's climate is less temperate than the rest of Europe, except in the north and northwest, where mild and wet conditions prevail, with 24 to 40 inches (61 to 102 cm) of rain a year and a median temperature of 47°F (8°C) in winter and 68°F (20°C) in summer.

In the inland regions of Spain, where summers are hot and rainfall is sporadic (as little as 14 inches or 36 cm per year), winters are cold. There, temperatures of 37°F (3°C) in winter are common, and summer temperatures can reach 80°F (27°C). Along the Mediterranean coastal region, and in Andalusia and the Balearic Islands, a summer drought, at times lasting up to five months, results in an annual rainfall of less than 24 inches (61 cm). Winter temperatures hover around 57°F (14°C), while in summer, they rise to 95°F (35°C). Snowfall in Spain is infrequent except in the mountains.

FLORA AND FAUNA

Spain's regional differences in geography and climate provide a rich variety of vegetation and animal life.

In Green Spain and the Pyrénées, dense forests (20% of Spain's land is forested) and grazing land form the perfect environment for mountain game, such as goats, boars, chamois, and rabbits, and birds like partridges and quails. A species of wild bear also lives here. The vegetation in these regions consists primarily of beech, oak, chestnut, eucalyptus, and smaller amounts of pine and fir. Apple orchards can be found along the base of mountain ranges in areas such as Asturias, and half-wild horses are said to roam the meadows of Galicia. This area is known for its abundance of seafood. Scallops, hake, salmon, and trout come from neighboring rivers and seas.

Citrus fruits, such as oranges, one of Spain's major exports, thrive in warm, sunny Valencia.

Along the Mediterranean coast, seafood and shellfish of all types are also abundant. Rice fields dot Valencia's outskirts. Vineyards and olive groves, palm trees, and almond, fig, and citrus orchards are characteristic of the Mediterranean landscape. In the arid interior and southern regions of the country, evergreen trees, such as holm oak and cork oak thrive.

Along the southern edge of Spain, in Andalusia, the flora and fauna are typical of a subtropical climate. Olive groves, vineyards, and fruit orchards (cherry, pear, peach, apricot, and almond) are common to the east. To the west, cotton, rice, and oranges are the predominant crops, and bulls are bred for the bullring. On the estuary of the Guadalquivir River lies Doñana National Park, one of the most important European

Almond trees in blossom. Besides citrus fruits and grapes, Spain produces many other fruits, such as apples, pears, almonds, apricots, figs, and peaches.

refuges for wild animals. Here, endangered wildlife such as the lynx and imperial eagle find shelter.

The Canary Islands' volcanic origins and African coastal climate produce interesting vegetation. The dragon tree, native to these islands, was once thought to be the source of dragon's blood, as the orange fruit of the tree contains a thick, red, inedible substance when dried. Even today, the tree seems mysterious, with its thick trunk and clusters of huge, broad, sword-shaped leaves. On the island of Tenerife, the oldest and tallest known dragon tree reaches a height of 70 feet (21.3 m). Extensive plantations of coffee, papaya, and banana are also common throughout the islands. A rare species of oleander grows in the center of the island of La Gomera. This variety of the green shrub, with its fragrant white or purple flowers, is considered a "living fossil," a remnant of a past geological age.

HISTORY

SPAIN'S LOCATION on the Iberian peninsula contributed to a history distinct from the rest of Europe. Mountain ranges and bodies of water separating Spain from the rest of the continent made for some resistance to, and isolation from, popular European culture and trends. On the other hand, its proximity to Africa led to invasions that brought rich cultural influences, and its proximity to the Atlantic Ocean gave Spain access to new territories in the Americas and immense wealth.

EARLY SPAIN

Evidence suggests that Spain has been inhabited for half a million years. Bones and tools of early humans have been found at Spanish sites, but the most impressive remains of Stone Age peoples are the polychrome paintings of bison, horses, and other animals on the ceilings of the caves at Altamira, painted by Homo sapiens some 15,000 years ago. Evidence of Copper Age culture exists in the south of Spain, where dolmens (megalithic tombs) were built. Many have survived.

From 1100 B.C., the earliest waves of immigrants from more advanced civilizations brought in new cultural influences. From the south and the Mediterranean came the Phoenicians, who colonized Cádiz and Almuñécar, and the Greeks, who made their settlements on the east coast (Málaga and Ampurias). From the north came the Celts, an Indo-European people who settled in the northwest and were later to have considerable influence in northern Spain. In 225 B.C., invading Carthaginians founded Cartagena, and eventually expanded their territory throughout much of the Iberian peninsula.

Opposite: **Dating from the fifth century B.C., the Lady of Elche, bust of an Iberian princess, is a fusion of early Greek and Iberian styles.**

Above: **Cave paintings at Altamira in northern Spain are among some of the most remarkable prehistoric paintings ever discovered.**

THE ROMAN CONQUEST

Rome invaded Iberia in 206 B.C. and defeated and expelled the Carthaginians. Over the next 200 years, the Romans gradually conquered the entire peninsula. Spain proved to be a valuable colony for Rome, as indigenous metals, such as gold, silver, copper, iron, tin, and lead, enriched the empire.

The Roman influence on Spain was more important, however. The present-day language, religion, and body of law all stem from this period of Roman domination, and many structures built by Roman engineers are still standing: the aqueduct of Segovia, the theater at Mérida, and the bridge of Córdoba.

VISIGOTHIC SPAIN

Early in the fifth century, Iberia was invaded by Germanic tribes. Among those who settled in Spain, the Vandals, who gave their name to Andalusia, and the Visigoths had the most influence. The Visigoths established a kingdom in the north, with Toledo as their capital, and the last Roman strongholds along the southern coast fell to the Visigoths by the seventh century. However, the Visigothic monarchy proved to be weak and, in A.D. 711, invading Muslims from North Africa swept into Andalusia and eventually destroyed the Christian Visigothic kingdom.

MUSLIM SPAIN

By A.D. 718, the Moors, as the Muslims were called by the Christians, controlled almost the entire Iberian peninsula. Many Christians converted to Islam, and Muslims of many nationalities—Arabs, Syrians, and Berbers—also settled in Spain, as the rich lands of southern Spain were attractive in comparison to the deserts of North Africa. The Moors renamed Andalusia, called Vandalusia by the Vandals, "al-Andalus." The barren highlands of Castile in central Spain were generally left unsettled.

AL-ANDALUS The independent Arab Muslim Umayyad dynasty of Spain ruled al-Andalus from 756 to 1031 from their capital at Córdoba. The reign of Caliph Abd-al-Rahman III (912–961) marked the height of economic and cultural splendor in Muslim Spain. Al-Andalus became a region of prosperous cities and intense trade.

Muslim rulers tolerated and encouraged religious and cultural diversity—Christians and Jews were permitted to worship as they pleased.

Greek philosophy was studied and spread throughout Europe, and great strides were made in astronomy, chemistry, and medicine.

The outer castle wall of the Moorish palace, Alhambra, at Granada. One of Spain's architectural masterpieces, Granada's magnificent Alhambra was the seat of Muslim rulers from the 13th century until 1492.

THE CHRISTIAN RECONQUEST The Muslims had allowed a few Christian territories to survive in the northern mountains, and these eventually grew into powerful kingdoms that started the reconquest of Moorish Spain. The regions of Navarre, Catalonia, Aragón, and Asturias became independent kingdoms by the 11th century, with Castile becoming the most important driving force behind the Christian reconquest. By 1248, only Granada remained a Muslim territory.

Muslim invasions from North Africa continued to threaten Christian Spain until the Christians finally completed their reconquest by taking Granada in 1492. Spanish unity was settled by the 15th century, although it would continue to be threatened by struggles for regional autonomy.

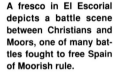

A fresco in El Escorial depicts a battle scene between Christians and Moors, one of many battles fought to free Spain of Moorish rule.

SPAIN DURING THE 16TH CENTURY

In the 16th century, Spain became the most powerful nation in the world, owing to immense wealth from its New World colonies and its alliance with the powerful Hapsburgs. Then a series of long, costly wars and revolts, plus defeat of the Spanish Armada by the English in 1588, caused a steady decline of Spanish power in Europe.

SPAIN UNDER THE CATHOLIC KINGS When Isabella I, Princess of Castile, married Ferdinand II, heir to the throne of Aragón, the union of the two most important kingdoms in Spain was finally achieved. The "Catholic Kings," as they were called, began their joint rule in 1479, and Isabella immediately took steps to centralize power.

In 1480, the Spanish Inquisition was established, and by 1492, with the last Moorish outpost conquered, all Jews and heretics (anyone who did not follow the orthodox teachings of the Catholic Church) were expelled from Spain, thrusting Spain into a period of orthodox Catholicism that also spurred strong nationalist sentiment.

In 1492, the Italian explorer Christopher Columbus, sponsored by the Spanish crown, sailed to the Americas and inspired a wave of Spanish exploration and conquest in the "New World." Ferdinand and Isabella then turned their attention to acquiring other areas on the Iberian peninsula and parts of Italy. In 1516, after the deaths of Ferdinand and Isabella, their grandson, Charles I, assumed the throne of both kingdoms, inaugurating the Hapsburg dynasty and Spain's Golden Age.

THE HAPSBURG MONARCHS For the next two centuries, the fate of Spain was tied to the Hapsburg dynasty. In 1519, Charles was elected Holy Roman Emperor (as Charles V) and departed for Germany. Charles

Tomb of Christopher Columbus in the Cathedral of Seville.

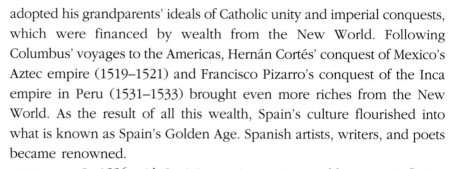

adopted his grandparents' ideals of Catholic unity and imperial conquests, which were financed by wealth from the New World. Following Columbus' voyages to the Americas, Hernán Cortés' conquest of Mexico's Aztec empire (1519–1521) and Francisco Pizarro's conquest of the Inca empire in Peru (1531–1533) brought even more riches from the New World. As the result of all this wealth, Spain's culture flourished into what is known as Spain's Golden Age. Spanish artists, writers, and poets became renowned.

In 1556, with Spain's ever-increasing wealth causing inflation and a decrease in domestic industry, Charles abdicated in favor of his son, Philip II, who inherited the rule of Spain, Sicily, and the Netherlands. Philip II proceeded to lead the cause of the Counter-Reformation against Protestant states in Europe. In 1588, he attempted to invade Protestant England by sea with his "Invincible Armada" but was defeated. This defeat marked the beginning of the decline of Spanish power.

DECLINE OF SPANISH GLORY

By the end of the 16th century, the economic and political glory of Spain had declined drastically, and the cultural leadership of Europe had passed to France.

A series of weak kings and ambitious ministers contributed further to Spain's downfall. The Thirty Years' War (1618–1648) began as a series of religious disputes but turned into a struggle between the Hapsburg and French Bourbon dynasties, each vying for control of Spain, weakening Spain in the process. Hapsburg rule finally ended in Spain with the reign of Charles II (1665–1700).

Statue of Philip III, son of Philip II, in Plaza Mayor, Madrid. His reign saw the decline of Spain as a great European power. Philip III took bad advice and expelled the Moriscos (Christians of Moorish ancestry), who had contributed much to Spain economically.

THE SPANISH BOURBONS The 18th century began with the War of Spanish Succession (1701–1714) by which French king Louis XIV acquired some Spanish territory and put his grandson, who became Philip V, on the throne. The early Bourbon rulers in Spain paid great attention to economic development and the centralization of power. By the mid-1700s, Spain experienced increased prosperity and unity, eventually becoming a union of provinces instead of a collection of kingdoms, as it had been throughout its history.

With the introduction of rational and enlightened ideals, in part learned from France, Spain moved away from its strong religious orientation. By 1767, the Jesuits were expelled, and the powers of the Inquisition reduced. In later years, Spain allied itself with France and was thus thrust into the Seven Years' War (1756–1763) against Great Britain.

FRENCH REVOLUTION AND NAPOLEONIC PERIOD Spain's decline in subsequent years invited intervention by other powers, notably the French. In 1793, during France's revolutionary wars, Spain was made a French outpost. Resentment turned against the throne and government, further weakening Spain.

In 1808, Napoleon Bonaparte forced the king of Spain, Charles IV, to abdicate in favor of his own brother Joseph Bonaparte. The Spanish rebelled against French occupation and were eager to adopt their own form of government. A democratic constitution was drawn up, whose progressive principles were disputed by liberals and conservatives for another 100 years. Efforts of the British and Spanish then forced France to evacuate, and in 1814, the Spanish throne was restored with the return of Ferdinand VII.

In 1540, St. Ignatius of Loyola founded the Jesuits, sparking the Counter-Reformation—a period of intense Catholic piety that was to dominate Spanish life for centuries.

1814 TO THE PRESENT

Spain was devastated by war and the loss of colonies in the New World. The rest of Europe was industrializing rapidly while Spain remained undeveloped and backward in comparison. Economic stability was impeded for decades.

PERIOD OF TROUBLES (1814–1875) Internal conflicts ensued as efforts toward a more liberal government were defeated by the autocratic Ferdinand VII. Quarrels over succession to the throne led to the Carlist Wars in 1833, sparking an era of upheaval. Military, peasant, and socialist uprisings, revolts of Carlists and federalists, and instability of the government, which alternated between monarchy and republic for several years, threatened to tear Spain apart.

The monument to Alfonso XII inside Retiro Park, Madrid.

BOURBONS RESTORED The First Spanish Republic was declared in 1873, and in 1874, Alfonso XII, a Bourbon, became king. His reign was marked by free trade. By 1890, however, with the declaration of universal suffrage for men, republicanism was again a growing force.

By 1897, the peaceful period had ended. A popular but conservative political leader, Antonio Canovas del Castillo, was assassinated, and in 1898, Spain lost the last of its empire in the Americas and the Pacific—Cuba, Puerto Rico, and the Philippines—in the Spanish-American War.

Domestic problems, bitter war in northern Morocco, and increased unrest led to the dictatorship of General Miguel Primo de Rivera in 1923. The general, who modeled his government on Italian fascism, was at first popular, but his attacks on liberals and his economic mismanagement forced him to resign in 1930, leaving Spain in the hands of King Alfonso XIII. In 1931, following the election of a Republican-Socialist government, Alfonso abdicated and left the country.

Nationalist leader General Francisco Franco, who overthrew the Spanish democratic republic in the Spanish Civil War.

REPUBLIC AND CIVIL WAR The Second Republic (1931–1939) brought about increased political participation in Spain but in so doing created conflict. Spain became divided into two opposing factions. On the right were the military, the church, landowners, and many small farmers, and on the left workers, landless peasants, intellectuals, and most Catalans and Basques. Some positive reforms were instituted during the first two years of the Republic, but eventually violent disputes between the left and the right (the liberals and the conservatives, respectively) led to the Spanish Civil War (1936–1939). General Francisco Franco led

The Valley of the Fallen commemorates the Civil War dead. Carved out of a mountain, it houses a basilica, a monastery, and General Franco's tomb. The top of the cross is 500 feet (152.3 m) above its granite base.

the right-wing nationalist movement, aided by Italian and German fascists, and quickly conquered the western half of Spain. The Republicans, despite some Soviet aid, were weakened by internal divisions and eventually fell to Franco's army. The tragic war cost Spain hundreds of thousands of lives, and many Spaniards fled the country.

Franco ruled the devastated nation as a military dictator for the next 36 years, supported by the Catholic Church and the Falange—the official fascist state party. He proved to be a stern ruler. Although his regime began as a repressive, totalitarian system, Franco set up his own brand of fascism, unlike the German and Italian models. Spain survived World War II by remaining neutral as it had in World War I, and this brought about negative feelings toward Spain by the Allies.

AFTER FRANCO In 1947, Spain declared itself a monarchy, with a king to be named to succeed Franco. In 1955, it became a member of the United Nations. Spain was still in a state of severe economic distress, and in the 1960s, Franco took steps to liberalize the economy. In 1969, Franco named the exiled Prince Juan Carlos I de Bórbon as his successor and heir to the vacant Spanish throne. After Franco's death in 1975, King Juan Carlos I, having sworn to uphold Francoist ideals while Franco was still alive, immediately started to generate democratic reform and guided Spain toward political liberalization with the help of new prime minister Adolfo Suárez González.

The first free general elections in 40 years were held in 1977. In 1978, a new constitution was put in place, restoring civil liberties and freedom of the press. In 1979, the parliament of Spain, the Cortes, approved provisional limited autonomy for Spain's regions, including Catalonia and the Basque provinces. Two attempted military coups, in 1981 and 1982, were easily suppressed, but Spain suffered from continued unrest, due mostly to terrorist activity from Basque separatists. Efforts consistently failed to bring peace to the region.

Spain's new government was very keen to create closer ties with the West. Negotiations to join the European Community (EC) began in 1976 and culminated in Spain's entrance in 1986. Spain joined NATO in 1982. That same year, the Socialist party won a majority in national elections, and their leader, Felipe González Márquez, was sworn in as prime minister. Socialists continued to win more victories in municipal and regional elections, and in 1993, González won an unprecedented fourth term as premier.

Below: **Felipe González Márquez, Spain's prime minister.**

Bottom: **The historic signing of the European Community Treaty, which made Spain a member.**

GOVERNMENT

SPAIN HAS COME a long way in becoming the democratic country it now is. In the 36 years of General Franco's military dictatorship, Spain suffered from restrictions of civil liberties and political activity, a repressed economy, and ostracism by most of the world. Spain was not permitted to become a member of the United Nations until 1955, and of NATO until 1982. The 1950s and 1960s saw a relaxation of political and administrative controls, but only after persistent cries for change. The unrest continued. In 1969, having declared years before that Spain would be restored to a monarchy upon his death or retirement, Franco nominated Prince Juan Carlos I de Bórbon, the grandson of the last reigning monarch, King Alfonso XIII, as heir to the throne. In November 1975, two days after Franco's death, the monarchy was reinstated, and Juan Carlos I was sworn in as king.

Opposite: **Rebuilt in the mid-1700s, Madrid's Royal Palace is now used for state functions.**

THE KING

Juan Carlos I was born on January 5, 1938, and lived in exile until coming to Spain to be appointed monarch. He is the eldest son of Don Juan, Conde de Barcelona. In an agreement between Don Juan and General Franco in 1954, Juan Carlos was given precedence as pretender to the Spanish throne and in 1975, was sworn in as king.

In 1966, Prince Juan Carlos married Princess Sophia of Greece, daughter of the late King Paul of the Hellenes and Queen Frederika of Greece. They have three children—two daughters and a son, Felipe, now Prince of Asturias, who in 1986, on his 18th birthday, was formally invested as heir to the Spanish throne.

A NEW ERA FOR SPAIN

King Juan Carlos and his appointed prime minister Adolfo Suárez González moved energetically to reform and liberalize the political system. Political parties were legalized in 1976, and free general elections were held in 1977. In 1978, parliamentary democracy began with the Constitution of 1978, the eighth constitution since 1812.

THE CONSTITUTION OF 1978

The constitution adopted in 1978 was an important step for Spain in many ways, as it succeeded in sweeping away the repressive remains of the Franco regime.

Among other things, the constitution restored civil liberties and freedom of the press, speech, and association; abolished torture and the death penalty; extended the right to vote beyond family heads to all citizens over 18 years of age; disestablished Roman Catholicism as the official religion; and paved the way for the reorganization and recognition of all provinces and their respective and unique heritage.

King Juan Carlos I played a pivotal role in transforming Spain from a military regime into a parliamentary democracy.

The Constitution of 1978 describes Spain as a hereditary, constitutional monarchy with a parliamentary form of government. Executive power rests with the king, prime minister, and Council of Ministers, or cabinet.

EXECUTIVE POWER

THE KING The king serves as the head of state, commander-in-chief of the armed forces, and symbol of Spain's "unity and permanence." Upon the king's death or abdication, the crown passes to the eldest son, or if there is no male heir, the eldest daughter.

The monarch exercises certain executive powers, drawing on the advice of the prime minister and the Council of Ministers. Royal involvement in state affairs must be approved by parliament, the Cortes.

PRIME MINISTER The prime minister, appointed by the monarch on the advice of the Council of Ministers, acts as the head of the government, directing Spain's domestic, foreign, and military policies with the aid of the Council of Ministers.

Felipe González Márquez is the current prime minister and has been since 1982. He is also the secretary-general of the Spanish Socialist Workers Party (PSOE), the largest political party in the legislature.

THE COUNCIL OF MINISTERS The Council of Ministers (cabinet) is recommended by the prime minister and appointed by the king. The Council of Ministers assists the prime minister and reports to the lower house of the legislature, the Congress of Deputies, for their policies.

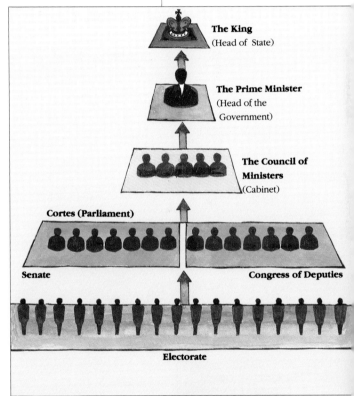

The Spanish system of government. Spain is a constitutional monarchy with a parliamentary form of government.

LEGISLATURE

Legislative power is invested in the parliamentary Cortes Generales, consisting of the very influential Congress of Deputies and the less powerful Senate. The Congress of Deputies has 350 members, elected proportionately according to the population of each province. The Senate has 208 directly elected members and 49 regional representatives from the mainland and island provinces and from Ceuta and Melilla, the Spanish enclaves in Morocco. Elections are held for both the Congress of Deputies and the Senate every four years.

JUDICIARY

Spain's judicial system is headed by the Supreme Court, or Tribunal Supremo, and includes territorial, provincial, regional, and municipal courts. The president of the Supreme Court, appointed by the king, also presides over the General Council of Judicial Power (CGPJ), formed by 20 members representing each facet of the judicial system (magistrates, judges, and attorneys). Members of the CGPJ govern all judicial power independent of the Cortes and the executive powers and are appointed by the Cortes and the king for five-year terms.

The Supreme Court is the highest authority in all questions of law, except constitutional issues, for which the Constitutional Court was established. Consisting of 12 members appointed by the king and serving a nine-year term, the Constitutional Court is wholly responsible for the interpretation of the constitution: laws and regulations; violations of fundamental and individual rights; and conflicts between the state and autonomous regions. The jury system was established by the constitution in 1978, but has yet to be applied.

Interior of the Congress Building.

LOCAL GOVERNMENT

Spain is divided into 50 administrative provinces (including the Balearic and Canary Islands), each with its own civil governor and elected local council that in turn elects mayors of cities and towns.

The Constitution of 1978 also provides for the establishment of 17 autonomous regions, in addition to the provinces, in an effort to recognize, preserve, and respect the common and historic characteristics of each region. It was most notably the strong demands from Basque and Catalan separatists that led to the creation of this system of regional self-government.

In 1979, the statutes of the first of the 17 Autonomous Communities were formalized, and the first parliaments were elected in the Basque and Catalan regions in 1980, followed by Galicia in 1981 and Andalusia in 1982. By 1983, the process was completed throughout all remaining 13 regions. These regional governing bodies work within the framework of Spain's constitution, national laws, and policy. Certain powers are delegated to them, such as the election of regional legislatures and presidents, responsibility for land use, public works and transportation, agricultural development, tourism, social and health aid, and the right to speak and practice different languages and cultural traditions.

A local council building in Seville, Andalusia. Greater autonomy is now given to local governments.

33

ECONOMY

UNTIL RECENTLY, Spain's economy lagged far behind that of its Western European neighbors. Having been quite slow to industrialize during the 18th and 19th centuries—the periods of great growth in industry for other countries—Spain remained primarily agricultural through the first half of the 20th century. Spain's Civil War brought about tragedy, devastation, great losses in the country's work force, worldwide isolation, and with that, economic depression. In the late 1950s, Franco attempted to make Spain more self-sufficient by reducing foreign imports and expanding domestic industry.

Opposite: **A stamp dealer attends to a tourist. Tourism is a major revenue earner in Spain.**

Below: **The harbor and port of Barcelona, Spain's major Mediterranean port and commercial center.**

35

The state-run National Industrial Institute (INI), set up to supplement private investment in areas of national interest, turned out to be a wasteful enterprise that encouraged inefficient industry and caused very high inflation rates. In 1959, Franco implemented a stabilization program that marked a turning point in Spain's economy, liberalizing trade and foreign investment. Spain made strong progress with a series of economic development plans, but per capita income was still far below that of many European countries. Spain, like many other countries, was hard hit by the oil price increases of 1973 and 1979. Many industries suffered during the late 1970s and early 1980s when industrial output growth was only 1%.

Perhaps the single most profound addition to Spain's economic improvement plan was the country's admission to the EC in 1986, which helped sustain economic growth for several years. However, in 1991, economic growth began to slow down, due, in part, to sustained high inflation rates. By early 1993, the Spanish economy was in recession. While Spain has begun to emerge from recession in 1994, recovery has, thus far, been slow.

Unemployment remains a serious problem for the Spanish government. In 1992, 18.4% of its labor force was unemployed, and more than a third of young Spaniards, aged 16–24, were out of work. The unemployment rate is expected to rise to over 20% for 1994 and 1995.

As Spain industrializes, factories with modern equipment, such as this knitwear plant, enable the country to compete with other industrial nations.

SPAIN'S ECONOMIC MIRACLE

In 1950, Spain was a devastatingly poor country, weakened by the Civil War, poor agricultural production, and isolation from foreign investment. In 1953, Franco signed a pact with the United States, granting U.S. forces the right to establish military bases on Spanish soil in exchange for foreign aid and arms. The result of this agreement was far-reaching.

Military and civilian personnel poured into Spain, and with them came American dollars and tourists. Spain at long last had the funds necessary to rebuild its crumbling economy. In 1955, Spain was accepted into the United Nations, thereby attracting more foreign investment. Franco's Stabilization Plan of 1959, a plan that increased domestic productivity and efficiency and liberalized foreign trade, readied Spain even more for the economic boom that was to come in the 1960s.

High industrial growth rates led to the creation of a new and prosperous middle class and brought increasing financial stability to the working class.

MANUFACTURING AND MINING

About 35% of Spain's labor force is employed in manufacturing, mining, and construction, which contribute roughly 38% of the Gross Domestic Product (GDP). Basic industries, such as iron and steel, shipbuilding, machine tools, and metallurgy, are located in the north of Spain in Bilbao, Santander, and Oviedo. Equally as important, manufacturing industries, such as plastics, rubber, textiles, and electronics, are located in Catalonia. A small concentration of industry occurs in Madrid, generally light chemical industry and high technology. Leather goods and shoes are produced in the Alicante province and in the Balearic Islands, and toys in Barcelona. Spain is also a large exporter of automobiles.

The most valuable minerals mined are mercury, anthracite, coal, lignite, sulfur, potassium, fluorspar, lead, and zinc. Both natural gas and crude petroleum are produced in small quantities. To lessen Spain's dependence on imported oil, the production of alternative sources of energy has increased dramatically in the past decade. In fact, expanded nuclear power capabilities provided 35.4% of Spain's electricity in 1991.

Spain boasts more vineyards than any other country. The growing demand for Spanish wines has led to an increase in grape production.

AGRICULTURE

The importance of agriculture within the Spanish economy has declined in recent decades. In 1950, more than half of Spain's work force was employed in agriculture, compared to about 10% today. Agriculture now contributes only about 5% to the GDP annually. About a third of the country's land is cultivated, with grains—most notably wheat and barley—occupying more than 60% of the cultivated area. Olive groves and vineyards also cover large areas, making Spain the world's largest producer of olives and olive products and the fourth largest producer of wines. Other important crops are citrus fruits, vegetables, sugar beets, cotton, and tobacco.

Spain's rough, irregular terrain and meager rainfall have contributed to the rather low productivity of agriculture. Irrigation, used extensively in drier regions, and technological advances in cultivation are helping to create more diversified farming. Livestock production is generally weak in Spain, although 27% of the cultivated land is used for pasture and meadow. Sheep and pigs are the two most important animals raised for meat.

FORESTRY AND FISHING

Traditionally, fishing has always been a significant industry for Spain. Its fishing fleet is one of the largest in the world. The main fishing region is in the northwest of Spain, most notably Galicia. Hake, anchovies, sardines, cod, and tuna are important catches, along with various mollusks and crustaceans.

Spain also has 38.8 million acres (15.7 hectares) of forest. Lumber, cork, resin, and Spanish hemp are the leading forest products.

TOURISM

The tourism industry is a major source of revenue for Spain, one of the leading tourist destinations in Europe.

Spain claims over 53 million visitors per year, who pour $18 billion into the economy. The destinations for these visitors are concentrated mostly along the Mediterranean coast. The majority of foreign visitors are from France, Portugal, Germany, Britain, and Morocco.

A fisherman in Galicia gets ready to cast his net.

FOREIGN INVESTMENT AND TRADE

Foreign investment has made very important contributions to Spain's economy and industrialization. An example is the auto industry.

The U.S. companies of Ford and General Motors have invested in the areas of Valencia, Saragossa, and Cádiz, making Spain the sixth largest exporter of cars in the world. Volkswagen, a German corporation, purchased SEAT, the Spanish automobile manufacturer, from the government. SEAT is today Spain's largest producer of automobiles and employs the greatest number of workers.

Spain's major trading partners are Germany, France, Italy, the United Kingdom, and the United States. Its main imports are petroleum products and mineral fuels, machinery, and electrical equipment. Exports include automobiles, fruit and vegetable products, iron, and steel goods.

THE SPANISH WORKDAY

The Spanish workday begins at 9 a.m., Monday through Saturday, although some businesses are closed all day Saturday. Most business people work until 1:30 p.m., and it is common to fill the morning hours with appointments and calls. Lunchtime is at 2 p.m., and the Spanish lunch is a leisurely one, whether surrounding a business occasion or not. Siesta, an afternoon nap or rest, is traditional in Spain and is taken after a hearty midday meal. Whether one sleeps or not, all businesses close between 1 and 4 p.m. to accommodate this lull in the day. Most Spaniards then return to their offices, where they work until 8 or 9 p.m.

Spanish business people are generally conservative and take their work seriously. They invariably show respect for a person of higher rank or position and will never argue or voice disagreement in direct language, as honor takes precedence over all else.

In 1992, Spain's Gross Domestic Product (GDP) was $515 billion, growing at an annual rate of 1%. The per capita income was $12,400.

Women who work in offices typically wear tailored dresses or blouses and skirts. Men wear jackets and ties, no matter what the temperature outside.

However, as formal and reserved as they are about dress, position, and integrity, Spaniards are more casual about time. It is not only common but acceptable to arrive 15–30 minutes late for a business appointment. A person who arrives on time may be thought to be too eager or even slightly aggressive.

It is also not the Spanish way to discuss business at the first meeting. The initial introduction is more an opportunity for both parties to get to know each other. Business contacts are more readily cultivated among friends.

More than nine out of every ten Spaniards live and work in cities and towns.

SPANIARDS

SPAIN HAS A POPULATION of roughly 39 million, distributed unevenly around the country. Having traditionally been a rural, agricultural society, Spain is now becoming more and more urbanized. Since the 1950s, more than five million people have left the predominantly impoverished rural regions and small towns of the west and south for the more industrial cities, such as Madrid, Barcelona, and Bilbao. A significant number also left Spain for more prosperous countries in Western Europe, including Switzerland, France, and Germany.

Spain is composed of diverse ethnic and linguistic groups whose presence and struggles for independence and recognition have sometimes been a disruptive force. In many instances, a Spaniard's loyalty is first to his or her *patria chica* ("pah-TREE-ya CHEE-kah"), or native region, and then to Spain. It has not always been easy for the government of Spain to recognize these differences and loyalties, however. Repressed during much of the Franco years, these regional communities were given more recognition in the 1978 constitution, which guarantees autonomy for the diverse nationalities that make up Spain. Although Castilian Spanish is still the official language of Spain, the constitution recognizes the distinct local languages and declares them co-official with Castilian Spanish for governmental purposes.

Opposite: **In rural areas such as Lanzarote, elderly Spanish women still dress conservatively in traditional black.**

Above: **Founded more than 3,000 years ago by the Phoenicians, Almuñécar is both a fishing village and a holiday resort. Two young inhabitants of Almuñécar show their entrepreneurial flair.**

THE PRINCIPAL ETHNIC GROUPS

The principal ethnic groups are the Catalans, who represent 17% of the population; the Basques, 2% of the population; and the Galicians, or Gallegos, who make up 7% of the total population. Other groups include the Valencians, Navarrese, Aragonese, and Gypsies.

THE CATALANS The region of Catalonia, comprising the provinces of Barcelona, Lérida, Tarragona, and Gerona, is the homeland of the Catalans (although in the Balearic Islands, parts of Valencia, and Aragón, there also exist Catalan-speaking populations).

A Catalan fishwife displays her wares. Known for their business spirit, Catalans are practical-minded and thrifty.

The site of many invasions and wars long ago, Catalonia has a rich history. The region became part of a united Spain during the reign of Ferdinand and Isabella. Hundreds of years later, during the Civil War, there existed for a short time a very proud "Catalan Republic," which also served as a home base for many of the era's anarchists and Communists. Although the independent republic did not survive the Franco years, autonomy for this region has never ceased to be an issue, and Catalans are second only to the Basques in their persistence for recognition.

The latter part of the 19th century saw renewed cultural pride and a sort of renaissance for the Catalans. Several criteria were used to distinguish Catalans from other Spaniards. Loyalty to Catalonia and its culture was probably the most important, along with the ability to speak the language.

What began in the last century continues today, as emphasis is on the Catalan language itself as the key to cultural distinctiveness. The educational policy of the region is that all students should be bilingual in Catalan and Castilian, but today, more schools teach classes in Catalan than they do in Castilian.

The Catalan region is prosperous, industrialized, and thoroughly urbanized, and Catalans are noted for their business sense, entrepreneurial skills, and thrift.

THE BASQUES The Basque country incorporates the provinces of Álava, Vizcaya, and Guipúzcoa, collectively known as "Euzkadi" by Basque nationalists. No one knows for sure how the Basques came to settle in this remote region of Spain, but what is known is that they are among the earliest people to inhabit Europe. They are by nature a fiercely independent people, proud of their difficult, mysterious language and rural culture.

Basques were great warriors and were the only people in Spain never totally brought under control by the Romans. By the Middle Ages, they were still largely untouched by the rest of European history and activity. Integrated into the kingdom of Castile in the 16th century, the Basques still managed to retain some privileges and exemptions by virtue of their cultural uniqueness.

In the 20th century, Franco put great effort into repressing Basque culture, especially the use of the language. Today, the Basque spirit lives on, perhaps the worst example of which is in the terrorist violence from separatist groups fighting for total independence from the Spanish government.

The Basque region is one of the most prosperous in Spain. Its metal, steel, and shipbuilding industries attract migrant workers from the inland and southern regions of Spain.

A Basque with the ubiquitous beret.

THE GALICIANS The provinces of La Coruña, Lugo, Orense, and Pontevedra make up the region of Galicia in the northwest corner of Spain. The region is sparsely populated as it is quite rural, and no real industry exists. Almost one million people have migrated out of Galicia to Spain's urban centers since the beginning of this century. Galicians are descended from early Celtic invaders who came from Northern Europe and settled in Galicia between 1000 B.C. and 600 B.C.

A bagpiper in Galicia. Galicians have more of a Celtic heritage than other Spaniards and are noted for their blond hair and light eyes.

In the middle of the 19th century, Galician nationalism was built around a tale of the region's Golden Age during the Middle Ages. While a kingdom did exist, it was short-lived. The southern part of the kingdom eventually became Portugal, and the northern portion was in complete disorder until 1483, when it was incorporated into the kingdom of Castile.

Modern-day nationalist movements date from 1931, but Galician efforts for autonomy pale in comparison to the more aggressive demands of both the Catalans and Basques.

Almost 60% of Galicia's population can claim authentic Galician ethnicity. Many still use the Galician language, but mostly at home. The language is more widely used in rural communities than in urban centers.

Galicians are, by trade and tradition, fishers, shepherds, and farmers. They are largely poor and conservative.

GYPSIES

Gypsies make up a small ethnic group in Spain, and their origins are generally unknown. It is thought that they migrated from Iran or India to Europe as early as the 11th century and arrived in Spain as early as the 15th century. No one really knows how many gypsies live in Spain today, as they are nomadic and a census is difficult to take. It is estimated that anywhere between 50,000 and three million live in all of Europe.

Upon their arrival in Spain in the 1400s, the gypsies were well received, but during the Spanish Inquisition, the gypsies, along with the Moors and the Jews, were driven out or forced to assimilate. Under Franco, persecution persisted, and by the 1980s, gypsies were still identified as an underclass. Recent reforms and special programs, however, are under way to promote education in the gypsy communities and to bring them more into the mainstream of Spanish and European life. Care is being taken not to eliminate their distinctive cultural traditions in the process.

Spanish gypsies are divided into two groups. The *gitanos* ("gee-TAH-nos") generally live in southern and central Spain, and most make a living as street entertainers or vendors. They are predominantly poor and uneducated, but well integrated into society. The *húngaros* ("HOONG-gah-ros") come from Central Europe, are much poorer than the *gitanos,* and live an almost entirely nomadic lifestyle, pitching tents and shacks around large cities for a short time.

A needy gypsy mother tries to make ends meet.

47

CLASS STRUCTURE

Class structure and social hierarchies are changing in Spain, as the country becomes more and more industrialized. Like Spain's Western European neighbors, Spanish society is increasingly differentiated along occupational and professional lines. The upper class consists of wealthy professionals and large landowners, who together make up roughly 13% of the population. The upper middle class, which includes technical professionals, owners of small businesses, and midlevel public and private employees, constitutes 36.3% of the population. The lower middle class—16.5% of the population—is made up of less-skilled workers and farmers. Spain's middle class is expanding, and the rural poor are decreasing.

In the small villages of the Meseta and the north, where most inhabitants own land that they themselves work, there are fewer differences in class and status. The population there is less likely to see people according to jobs and economic earnings and more likely to feel bound to one another by religion and kinship. Also, as modernization comes to these villages, the gaps in material possessions between rich and poor disappear. Each person is just as likely to own a car, television, or refrigerator as any other. However, this sense of community is not the case in the agricultural towns of Andalusia. There, where the land is unevenly distributed and worked by day laborers, class delineation is sharply evident and class conflicts quite obvious.

DRESS

Spaniards today dress much like Western Europeans and Americans. There was a time when Spanish women wore heavy black clothes, but now, only the older generation in isolated, rural areas dress this way.

Living standards in Spain have improved dramatically in the last 20 years. In 1969, there were 113 telephones per 1,000 inhabitants. By 1992, the figure had risen to 357 telephones.

Certain areas of Spain, such as Madrid, Barcelona, and Málaga, are becoming quite important in the fashion world, and the more stylish inhabitants of these cities could rival any chic Parisian or American.

Generally, for most Spaniards, conservative dress is the norm. General business attire is seen on office workers and professionals. Students wear jeans, baggy sweaters, and whatever else attracts their eye, as most students of all Western cultures do. Agricultural and factory workers, of course, dress to suit the physical requirements of their work. Shorts are not worn in public much, except for beach and resort areas.

Spaniards in elegant attire enjoy the mild winter sun in a park in Barcelona.

LIFESTYLE

AS VARIED AS SPAIN IS, in terms of geography, climate, and culture, there still exists a distinct, national personality that links all the many different peoples and cultures of Spain into one. Spaniards are gay and vivacious, evident in their readiness to enjoy a festival and partake in celebrations. They are passionate about the arts, their family, and their faith, and their pleasures are modest. A good meal, a sunny courtyard filled with flowering plants, the company of beloved family and friends, a relaxing siesta, and a hearty laugh—these are the makings of Spanish life.

Opposite: **Whether it is at a café by the castle wall or in a restaurant, Spaniards eat and entertain out whenever they can.**

Below: **Young Spanish women participating in a festival.**

51

Religion, politics, and affairs of the heart are subjects of discussion generally avoided until a more intimate relationship develops.

SOCIAL CUSTOMS

Spaniards are at ease with themselves and their world, but they do adhere to certain social graces. Invitations to the home of a friend are considered an honor, as Spaniards do not generally open their home to anyone but family and very close friends. Guests rarely refuse invitations (to do so without just cause would be an insult) and bring with them flowers, sweets, or gifts for the children.

In greeting, Spaniards show affection and warmth, shaking hands upon first meeting, and kissing each other on the cheek when they leave. They are expected to engage in pleasant conversation, staying away from controversial confrontation unless they know each other well.

Recognition of rank is taken for granted in Spain, whether in the home, office, or everyday life. Children do not openly defy or show disrespect to their parents by talking back or disobeying in public. In business, bosses or supervisors are treated with respect even when they falter; errors or embarrassments are never pointed out by a subordinate. In the world of business, ultimate respect takes the place of ambition.

In the past, when the lines between rich and poor were so sharply delineated, the opinions and actions of a wealthy landowner or official had terrific sway over those of a poor laborer or member of the rural lower class. As the middle class grows in Spain—and it will continue to do so with the government's far-reaching economic policies—these lines of social distinction are becoming more and more blurred.

No longer does a poor person automatically defer to someone who is rich. By constitutional decree, each has equal right to all that society has to offer: political voice, economic opportunities, education, and sources of pleasure.

SPANISH PRIDE

Spanish pride is legendary. Where else would El Cid, an opportunistic warrior, be a national hero; and Don Quixote, a fictitious half-crazed dreamer, the symbol of the Spanish noble cause? What other country would cheer a dying bull that fought bravely in the ring and boo the victorious matador who did not? The very fabric of Spanish life and the very essence of the Spaniards lie in their honor, their sense of dignity, and adherence to moral right and wrong.

A Spanish farm worker. Spaniards take much pride in their work.

Indeed these principles are evident today, as Spaniards take themselves and their efforts very seriously. Spaniards feel pride of birthplace, of region, and of culture. This is no more evident than in the regional separatist movements that have been around for centuries and are still quite active, especially among the Catalans and Basques. Efforts to restore the use of the regional languages in school, on public signs, and at home and to pass on cultural traditions to the next generation are widespread.

A Spanish man is a good father, husband, and provider. A Spanish woman keeps a clean house, makes sure the children are well-groomed and healthy, and if she works, as more and more women do, she does that too with efficiency and poise. It is said that a Spaniard would rather do a bad job well, than a good job poorly, and perhaps this is true. Ambition for the sole purpose of acquiring money is still not very commonplace. Perhaps this is one of the reasons it has taken Spain so long to develop into an international competitor, even considering the setbacks caused by the 36 years of Franco's rule.

EL CID: THE NATIONAL HERO

Ruy Díaz de Vivar, known as El Cid (which is derived from the Arabic word *sidi,* meaning leader or lord), was born in the town of Burgos in 1043. This historical figure was a warrior of questionable loyalty, but his victories made him famous. He fought against both Christians and Moors as it suited him, but his greatest triumphs were over the Moors. In 1094, El Cid captured Valencia from the Muslims and ruled there until his death five years later.

His exploits were made legendary in the Spanish epic *The Poem of the Cid*, written by an anonymous monk just 40 years after his death. El Cid will always be remembered for his dignity and courage. He fought and went to war for the sheer glory of it all and was victorious because of his own will and belief in himself. Many towns all over Spain still bear his name.

THE CONCEPT OF INDIVIDUALISM

The Spaniards have always asserted their uniqueness—that which sets them apart from each other and the rest of the world. They have always wanted to succeed by their own initiative, being unable to tolerate having ideas or dogma imposed on them. What a strange irony, then, that for so many years, Spain has been controlled and repressed by others. First by so many invasions—Roman, Visigoth, Moor—then again during the reign of the Catholic Kings when conformity was the key to survival and religious fanaticism the driving force. During the Franco years, individualism was hatefully discouraged, even punished. No wonder that so many liberals, artists, and freethinkers left Spain to pursue their lives elsewhere. Democratic freedom finally came to Spain, but its arrival was long overdue.

LIFE IN URBAN CENTERS

Between the last decade of the Franco regime and the first decade of a democratic government, Spain's population steadily migrated to urban areas. Today, roughly 91% of Spain's population live in urban areas, compared to 61% in 1965. The most populous city is Madrid, followed by Barcelona, Seville, and Valencia. As is the case with most big cities, such as Paris or New York, the inhabitants of Spain's metropolitan areas were often born elsewhere. Migrations from the rural areas to cities like Madrid and Barcelona make up for a large percentage of the total population of those cities, which are dominated by a growing middle or upper middle class. Many of these people in the cities work in administrative, clerical, or service industries.

The center of life in the city is usually the town center or square. Shopping areas, restaurants, offices, and theaters attract the most people. Traffic is heavy, especially during rush hour, but all hours of the night are a perfect time for traffic congestion, as Spain's big cities rarely sleep. Parking spaces are few and hard to find, and it is perfectly acceptable to squeeze a car into an illegal spot or to park on a sidewalk.

The Gran Vía is Madrid's main artery. Lined with shops, cinemas, cafés, and restaurants, it bustles with activity day and night.

A town house in the Basque region.

Housing is a big problem in Spain's metropolitan cities and has been since the migration to urban areas began.

In the 1960s, Spain's government called for a national housing plan, aimed at creating four million new dwellings within a 15-year period, but these efforts proved ineffective in the long run. Construction was focused on large, high-rise, moderately expensive apartment buildings, and the much-needed small, modest apartments were all but forgotten.

To make matters worse for the working class, most of these dwellings were for sale, not rent, making it almost impossible for the needy to find affordable, decent housing. Housing was not only scarce, it was also in poor condition—10% were classified as being in serious need of repair, and only 37% were equipped with modern amenities. In 1982, the Socialist government announced a plan to correct the housing problem in urban centers, aiming to give all citizens homes by the 1990s.

The majority of middle-class urban residents live in large, impersonal apartment complexes on the outer rims of the cities, where construction is generally flimsy and maintenance costs are high. For the lower classes, housing is located in shacks and shantytowns on the outskirts, with poor sanitation and lighting.

THE TRANSFORMATION OF RURAL AREAS

Today, 9% of Spain's total population live in the countryside and rural areas. This figure decreases steadily each year, as more and more of each new generation move away from the farm to pursue their lives in larger cities. In Spain, sons no longer follow the father in traditional occupations and lifestyles. Furthermore, the prestige of farming as a way of life is rapidly declining in rural areas. As Spain opens up to new ideas from the outside world, the traditional rural class becomes exposed to new alternatives in living and working, perhaps alternatives that were

In some rural areas, villages have been almost totally abandoned as the young have left to pursue more exciting lives in the city.

never possible before. In extreme cases, emigration to larger cities and greater opportunities was a matter of life or death. Many farmers were forced to sell their farms when faced with a particularly bad year, and they had to find alternative means of making a living elsewhere.

Tourism has played a role in making some rural villages less isolated. These areas have been improved somewhat by the construction of better roads, electricity, and other facilities for the tourist industry. Tourists are attracted to the natural resources that provide skiing, mountain climbing, and hiking in mountainous areas, and swimming and water sports in coastal villages. In these areas, tourism has replaced agriculture as the main source of revenue.

In some Basque villages, the traditional social structure has broken down as the value placed on farming has declined.

A farmer on his donkey cart.

In a small Castilian village called Navanogol, three hours west of Madrid, mass emigration led to revitalization, a higher standard of living, and the modernization of the village. Navanogol is different in that the variation of terrain makes working with mechanized tools and tractors almost impossible. Here, farming methods are not much different from those used long ago, and human labor is an important part of the process.

As day laborers left the area to work in Madrid and other cities, large landowners, deprived of their labor force, had to sell, rent, or sharecrop the land. Farmers and day laborers, who did not have the means before, now had the opportunity to control or own a piece of land. This led to increased prosperity among the vast majority of villagers. Also, relatives, especially children, who now worked in cities, would send a portion of their earnings, as well as clothes, appliances, and other modern amenities, back home. Home improvements have been substantial—dirt floors converted to cement, wood, or tile; open hearth ovens replaced by gas stoves; and radio or television in just about every home. There is a saying now in Spain, that "there aren't any poor people in Navanogol anymore."

EDUCATION

During the Franco years, most education was subsidized by the government and administered by the Catholic Church. The system was traditional, conservative, and authoritarian. Many levels of education, especially the higher and university levels, were available only to the upper classes, making it quite difficult for a member of the lower class or rural community to better himself or herself through education. This contributed to social, cultural, economic, and political differences between classes.

One of King Juan Carlos' first tasks when he came to power was educational reform, and it has been a major issue for the Socialist government ever since. The stated purposes of the country's educational system are cultural integration to encourage a unified nation, social integration to contribute to the integration of society, economic integration to create opportunities for all, and political integration to maintain democratic values.

Since 1991, when the General Regulation of the Educational System Act came into force, primary (for ages 6–11) and secondary (12–16) education has been free and compulsory. Secondary education terminates with the *bachillerato* ("bah-KEE-yay-RAH-toh"), an all-encompassing countrywide exam. Preparations for this examination cause much anxiety as it is essential for students to pass this examination in order to receive their diplomas. University or higher education is optional, but entrance examinations are compulsory if one chooses to attend. Spain is now experiencing a zeal for education as never before.

As a result of the government's educational reforms, nearly all children between ages six and 16 are enrolled in primary and secondary school. In 1992, public expenditure on education took up 4.7% of the

Muslims founded the first Spanish university at Valencia in 1209. Spain's literacy rate now is 95% after years of vigorous effort by the government to accommodate all who desire an education.

country's Gross Domestic Product. Spain's literacy rate is now 95%.

The university system in Spain has undergone some changes as well. In 1983, the Socialist government sought to lessen the central government's control over the universities and their curriculum and gave each public university increased autonomy.

Students can choose a five- or six-year university program that offers liberal and professional studies, such as law, medicine, sciences, and humanities, or enroll in a technical college that offers degrees in engineering, architecture, industrial, and other applied skills, after three years of study.

In 1992, there were 1,194,000 students studying in Spain's universities. More students are enrolling in the professional and liberal study programs, seeking careers in medicine, law, and other professions. At present there are 43 universities in all of Spain, four of which are private Catholic universities. There is also an Open University based in Madrid that teaches by mail, radio, and television.

CHANGES IN ATTITUDES

During the 36 years of Franco's authoritarian and conservative rule, Spain was isolated from the rest of the world and essentially locked in the past, lagging well behind its Western European neighbors in terms

Students in deep concentration in a quiet corner of the Gothic quarter, Barcelona. The young today have more opportunities to determine their future.

of social and cultural developments. With the advent of democracy in today's Spain, however, freedom of expression and social and political changes have helped to create new opportunities and lifestyles for many of its people.

Although once cited as the most conservative country in Western Europe, Spain is decidedly becoming more and more liberal. Freedom of the press and the outlawing of censorship have spawned a host of newspapers, magazines, and literature reflecting the changes in social and political mores all over the world. Now that Spaniards are exposed to such literature, they have also adopted these changing progressive views, especially the young people. Socialist sentiments are popular among university students, and displays of affection are common in public.

More and more couples live together without being married. Divorce was not common during the Franco regime, as the Church opposed it,

the conservative government all but condemned it, and the process itself was fairly expensive. In the 1980s, however, 80% of Spanish people polled favored divorce and more than half, the use of contraception.

Today's youth are more familiar with computer games than with traditional games.

TODAY'S YOUTH

Young people of all classes are becoming avid consumers, spending most of their money on clothes, music, motor scooters, and evenings out at clubs.

This consumerism has helped to reduce class gaps among the youth, as distinctions by material possessions become increasingly less obvious. In addition, young people are knowledgeable and enthusiastic about American trends in music, fashion, and movies.

THE CHANGING ROLE OF WOMEN

The role of women is changing in Spain, as new opportunities and freedom arise. The country's dramatic industrialization programs have encouraged women to join the job market. In 1940, women represented less than 15% of the working population. Today, that figure has risen to nearly 40% and keeps rising. This has brought an increase in child-care centers and more liberal attitudes about the place of women in society, sociologically, politically, and legally.

Although poorer women have always worked, usually as domestics, they are now seeking more jobs in the service sector, as salespeople and

62

waitresses. Middle-class women are seeking jobs in technical fields, as pharmacists, clerks, and teachers. They generally work part-time and are paid less than their male counterparts for the same position. Many working women, however, do not want to give up the responsibility of their home or family life. It is not unusual for them to spread their time equally between their homes, children, and jobs, unwilling to relinquish either their newfound freedom or their long-held traditions.

A craftswoman gainfully employed in the exquisite art of lace-making.

Women are also assuming roles once reserved for men. More and more women are entering male-dominated fields, such as engineering, architecture, law, medicine, chemistry, and the social sciences. Women also work in libraries, museums, banks, publishing, healthcare, marketing, and, in the big cities, as police officers.

Changing identities are happening in all age groups. Young girls are joining the work force when they are able, working after school in offices and shops in order to contribute to the family income, and have enough money for clothes, makeup, movies, and other pastimes. Also, some middle-class women are finishing their education, returning to school after the children have left home.

Women have made progress in legal matters as well. During the more conservative years, women had almost no legal rights. They could not sign a legal document or receive a salary without their husbands' permission. A married woman had no right to an inheritance and was punished severely for adultery, while the man escaped punishment altogether.

RELIGION

ROMAN CATHOLICISM is the major religion of Spain, although the present constitution disestablished Roman Catholicism as the official religion and guaranteed religious freedom to all inhabitants. Roughly 99% of Spain's population identify themselves as Catholic. The remaining 1% belong to mainly Protestant groups, Jehovah's Witnesses, and Mormons, with small communities of Jews in larger cities, and Muslims near the southern coast.

THE HISTORY OF CATHOLICISM IN SPAIN

Catholicism has touched Spain like nowhere else and has been a strong force in the history of the country since it was first declared the sole religion by the Romans in A.D. 380. What has always differentiated Spanish Catholics from Catholics in other parts of the world is their uncompromising attachment to the Church and the religious dogma it preaches.

Strangely enough, although Spain's religious history has been shaped by the countless struggles between Catholicism, Islam, and Judaism, it is just these groups—the Muslims and the Jews—that inspired Spain to mix religious fervor with national sentiments.

As a result, religion became a weapon. This concept developed over centuries of crusading along the Iberian peninsula and culminated with the reign of the Catholic Kings, Isabella and Ferdinand, who held complete control over both religion and government. During the Middle Ages, when Spain was a collection of states, religion was the unifying force that held the kingdoms together.

Opposite: **A Catholic church in Alicante. Religion is an integral part of Spanish life.**

Below: **Pilgrims on the last leg of their journey to the Cathedral of Santiago de Compostela, Galicia. Containing the relics of St. James the Apostle, Santiago has been a shrine for pilgrims since the Middle Ages.**

The oldest synagogue in
Toledo, Santa Maria de la
Blanca was built in the
9th century. Toledo was
the capital of the Spanish
Jews between the 11th
and the 13th centuries. Of
the ten synagogues in
the city, only two survive.

The Catholic Kings took this a step further and sought to purge the peninsula of other religious groups by means of the Spanish Inquisition, a cruel, relentless crusade abolished in Spain only in the 1830s, outliving its strongest defenders, Isabella and Ferdinand, by over 300 years.

During the Franco years, the significance and privileges of the Catholic Church were restored. Catholicism, although officially declared the state religion in 1851 by a pact between the Vatican and the Spanish government, and renounced by the Republic in 1931, was again during Franco's regime the only religion to have legal status. No Protestant church, Jewish synagogue, or Muslim mosque was allowed to advertise services, identify its religious beliefs, own property, or publish literature, and religious mobs led countless attacks on differing places of worship. Franco had the power to appoint clergy, and his government directly subsidized the Church, paid priests' salaries, and reconstructed numerous church buildings damaged in the Civil War. In addition, Franco passed laws abolishing divorce and the use of contraceptives, and religious instruction was mandatory in all schools. Countless artists, liberals, and intellectuals left Spain during these years to escape Franco's repressive "church-state."

THE SPANISH INQUISITION

The Inquisition did not begin in Spain, but this is where it gained the most notoriety. Instituted in 1480, the Spanish Inquisition was a separate tribunal of the Roman Catholic Church designed to rid the country of "heretics," or those who went against the teachings of the Church. Set up by Ferdinand and Isabella, its primary tenets were:

- to offer protection to converted Jews, the *conversos* ("con-BER-sos"), from retaliation by hostile members of the Jewish faith and to make sure they didn't lapse back into Judaism;
- to seek out lapsed Jewish converts, called *marranos* ("mah-RAH-nos"), a term that also came to mean "secret Jew" or swine; *marranos* usually practiced their Jewish faith in private;
- to prevent the relapse of the converted Moors, called *moriscos* ("moh-REES-kos"), and to prevent them from forming "dangerous" alliances with other heretical groups.

Shortly after it began, however, the Spanish Inquisition was cited for numerous abuses. Accusations of heresy ran rampant, and innocent, faithful people were unjustly punished by public trial and condemnation. This usually took the form of strangulation or burning at the stake, and members of some Christian groups were sentenced to life in prison. Jews and Muslims were expelled or forced into Catholic conversion. The Spanish Inquisition, although vastly changed and more humane, remained a force in Spain until the early 19th century.

CATHOLICISM AND PRESENT-DAY SPAIN

King Juan Carlos I did much to lessen the importance of the Catholic Church in the everyday life of Spain. But although no longer the official religion, the Church still enjoyed a privileged status until only recently. Government financial support of the Church and church-affiliated schools had not ended by the late 1980s, and this led to much controversy among Socialist officials and party members.

In addition to government-imposed changes, there are many other forces at work helping to bring about changes between the Catholic Church and the people of Spain. The economic and demographic shift from a rural society to an urban one has contributed greatly to secularization. Traditionally, rural villages and small towns have celebrated and glorified the local church and clergy. But as Spain modernizes and adapts to industrialization and capitalism, religious faith among the people becomes less important because the Church has less influence over its members.

The increase in financial gain of most Spaniards means that they identify themselves more by materialistic means than by religious beliefs. To be a good Catholic is no longer synonymous with being a good or successful person, and to be a priest or clergy member in Spain is no longer the source of intense family pride as it was in the past. In fact, the number of Spaniards entering holy orders declined greatly in the 1980s.

OBSERVANCE OF CATHOLICISM

Today, to be a Catholic in Spain has more to do with religious observance of important rituals and celebrations than it does with regular attendance at mass. Few Spaniards attend mass on a regular basis, but many believe in Catholicism as a faith. Seven rituals of the Roman Catholic Church are central to observance of the religion.

A faithful Catholic kisses the feet of a statue of Jesus.

1. BAPTISM Baptism is symbolic of spiritual rebirth, when an individual is cleansed of all "original sin." Roman Catholics believe all humans are born deprived of grace as a result of Adam's sinful disobedience of God. Infants just days old are baptized, but followers of all ages can be baptized as well. In Spain, nearly 85% of all Catholics are baptized in church. The people in attendance, usually the parents, godparents, and other members of the family, dress formally. The infant wears a long white gown, usually passed down from generation to generation and treasured. Afterward, a hearty meal or celebration is common.

2. CONFIRMATION This sacrament admits a baptized person to full membership in the Catholic Church and in doing so, solidifies and strengthens his or her faith. A person is usually confirmed between the ages of 12 and 18, but a person of any age can be confirmed.

3. FIRST HOLY COMMUNION Also called the Eucharist, this sacrament commemorates Christ's Last Supper. At mass, Catholics come forward, kneel before the priest, and receive a sip of wine and a wafer, symbolizing the blood and body of Christ. Most Catholics take their First Communion when they are between six and 10 years old.

4. MATRIMONY Marriage in the Catholic Church occurs between two baptized persons and has two essential properties: unity—one spouse; and indissolubility—meaning that it is a contract for life. In Spain, nearly 90% of all marriages occur in the Catholic Church. Divorce was outlawed, not only by the Catholic Church throughout history, but also during Franco's regime. Since July 1981, however, divorce has been legal.

A Catholic priest at his office.

Seville's cathedral, La Giralda, is built on the remains of a mosque.

5. HOLY ORDERS This is the sacrament of ordination, by which one is admitted into the priesthood or ministry. Only men are allowed to be priests in the Catholic Church, and they must vow never to marry.

6. PENANCE This sacrament includes the act of contrition, which means having sincere remorse for having sinned; confession to a priest; acceptance of punishment; and absolution, which can only be imparted by a priest after punishment has been carried out. According to the Roman Catholic Church, all Catholics who have reached the age of reason should confess their sins at least once a year. These sins can range from simple wrongdoings like an act of vanity to serious ones, such as adultery. Sinners show repentance by carrying out punishments that usually take the form of a series of recitations and prayer. Absolution is then granted, and the sinner forgiven by God.

7. EXTREME UNCTION Also known as last rites, this sacrament is the last of the life cycle within the Catholic Church. A priest performs extreme unction by anointing the forehead with oil and praying for one who is very sick, usually when death is imminent. Extreme unction is assurance that the person who is dying will be absolved of all sins and able to enter heaven.

THE LEGACY OF THE CATHOLIC CHURCH

In Spain, there are countless examples of the glory that was the Catholic Church at its most powerful, the most obvious being the many cathedrals that grace the country. Over 40 cities in Spain boast outstanding cathedrals. The cathedral in Seville is the biggest and tallest in the country and the largest Gothic building in the world. But perhaps the most impressive religious building is the Mezquita, or grand mosque, at Córdoba, which was once both the Roman and Muslim capital of Spain.

Built over a period of 200 years, between the eighth and 10th centuries, the Mezquita began as a mosque built on the site of an earlier Visigothic church, some ornate details of which were preserved. The mosque contained an original copy of the Koran, the Islamic holy book, and a bone from the Prophet Mohammed, and it was a building of beauty and brilliance. In the 16th century, however, under the sanction of King Charles V, a baroque cathedral was built in the center of the glorious Muslim structure. Charles V later regretted his action when he saw how the construction was carried out and reportedly said, "You have built here what you, or anyone, might have built anywhere else; but you have destroyed what was unique in the world."

Interior of the Mezquita, Córdoba. The mosque, once one of the most important points of Muslim pilgrimage, was the site chosen by Charles V to build a baroque cathedral in the 16th century.

PLAZA DE TOROS DE
GIRONA
INAUGURADA EN 1897
Empresa: ALCALDE C.B.
ORGANIZACIÓN: AMADOR HERNÁNDEZ

DOMINGO
DIMANCHE
SUNDAY
SONNTAG
DOMENICA

31

Marzo
Mars
March
März
Marzo

1991

¡INAUGURACION DE LA TEMPORADA!

Tarde a las 5
A 17'00 h.
At 5.00 p. m.
Um 17 00 uhr.

PRESENTACION DEL MEJOR ESPECTÁCULO DE EUROPA

GRANDIOSA CORRIDA DE NOVILLOS TOROS Con picadores

6   6
Con permiso de la Autoridad y si el tiempo no lo impide, serán lidiados, picados, banderilleados y muertos a estoque

HERMOSOS Y BRAVOS NOVILLOS TOROS
de la acreditada ganadería de
SOTO DE LA FUENTE, de Sevilla (Guillena)
con divisa celeste y blanca
para los valientes matadores

JESUS SANJUAN
de Zaragoza

PACO SENDA
de Valencia

PACO AGUILERA
de Priego (Córdoba)

TAQUILLA OFICIAL:
Plaza de Toros - Tel. 20 28 96
GIRONA
TICKETS: Camping, Hotel, Agency

NOTAS: Las reglamentarias.
Las puertas de la Plaza se
abrirán 2 HORAS antes.

Una brillante banda de
música amenizará
el espectáculo

LANGUAGE

SPANISH IS ONE of the Romance languages spread by the Roman conquerors when Rome held power over most of the Western world. It began as a regional dialect, and through widespread usage became a formal language with grammatical rules and a literature of its own.

What the rest of the world knows as Spanish is called Castilian in Spain, as it was originally the dialect of the kingdom of Castile. Castilian is the official language of Spain, and all government business is conducted in this language. Castilian is spoken mostly in central Spain and is thought of as the most prestigious form of Spanish.

One in four Spaniards speaks a language other than Castilian, although the majority, roughly 74%, speak Castilian Spanish regularly. However, there are three important regional languages in Spain, each with its own structure, vocabulary, and literature: Catalan, Galician, and Basque. About 17% of Spaniards speak Catalan, while 7% speak Galician, and 2% speak Basque. All regional language speakers can and do speak Castilian. In addition to these three regional languages, there are also important dialects spoken throughout the country, such as those in Valencia and Aragón.

REGIONAL LANGUAGES

The language differences in Spain make for a frustrating time when one is traveling from one region to another. Road signs are sometimes in the language of the region, making it hard for travelers to understand if they are not familiar with the particular tongue. More important than that, however, is the fact that these language differences often create a rift among the people of Spain. The country has been threatened with partial division and related independence movements on numerous occasions, most notably by the Basques.

Opposite: **A poster announces details of a bullfight in Castilian. In Spain, Castilian Spanish is the official language. Catalan is widely spoken in the northeast, Galician in the northwest, and Basque in the north.**

An open-air bookstall in old Madrid. During the Franco years, regional language books and classics were destroyed.

During Spain's long history, many governments were not always tolerant of the language differences. Over the years, successive rulers have equated sameness of tongue with stability in government, and the regional dialects were frequently outlawed. Francisco Franco in particular was extremely severe on the subject. Under his regime, regional languages that had been permitted during the Second Republic were restricted in favor of Castilian. Literary classics and school books were burned, the publication of regional language newspapers was prohibited, and regional languages were banned from public office and establishments.

It was not until the 1960s that the government grew more tolerant. In Spain today, respect for all regional languages is encouraged. Many schools include in their curriculum regional languages and literature.

CATALAN Catalan is spoken in Catalonia, the region along the northeastern coast of the Mediterranean. Closely related to the Provençal language of southern France, Catalan is said to be actually closer to French in vocabulary and accent than to Castilian Spanish. One of the Romance languages, Catalan is derived from the rich languages of the Oc linguistic region in France and is especially suited to lyric poetry and song. More literature has been written in Catalan than in either Galician or Basque.

There are subtypes of the Catalan language, spoken in Valencia and the Balearic Islands, called Valencian and Balearic. And from Fraga southward, at the edge of Valencia, there is a zone where people speak a mixture of Castilian and Catalan, called *Chapurriao* ("CHAH-poo-ree-OW") from the Spanish verb *chapurrer,* meaning to jabber.

GALICIAN Galician is spoken in Galicia, on the northwestern coast of Spain. Given its proximity to Portugal, the regional language is closely related to Portuguese and was probably a Portuguese dialect spoken in this Spanish territory. Galician has its roots in the Romance languages. It is primarily a rural language and is not heard much in the larger cities of the region. Galician nationalists feel Galician should be given precedence over Castilian in schools, public offices, and business transactions.

BASQUE Of all the languages in the world, and certainly those spoken in Spain, Basque (called *Euskera* or "yoo-SKAY-rah" in Basque), spoken in the Basque Provinces of Spain, is unique. Thought to be spoken throughout the western and central Pyrénées regions in ancient times, Basque is now limited to Vizcaya, Guipúzcoa, and Álava, and parts of southwestern France.

While differences in the lifestyle and cultural traditions still exist, the process of assimilation of the Spanish population has gone on for such a long time that identification of Spain's ethnic groups will soon be based only on language.

Perhaps no other language has given so much trouble to linguistic scholars and philologists, as no one can trace the true origins of Basque. It is related to no other language except that of a small area in the Caucasus Mountains of the former Soviet Union. Its bizarre structure, compounding words to form new ones, has its echoes in prehistory. For instance, the Basque names for some weapons and tools contain stone as their root meaning. The word for knife translates as "stone-that-cuts;" a spear is "stone-stick," and the word for ceiling means literally "roof-of-the cave."

It is said that the Basque language can only be learned at "Mother's knee." In fact, its extremely difficult vocabulary and grammatical structure have elicited a Spanish proverb: "When God wanted to punish the Devil, he condemned him for seven years to study Basque." Basque is not part of the formal curriculum in

Two Galician women converse.

Spanish schools, but is spoken in the small villages, towns, and farmsteads of the provinces, where families try to keep the language alive from generation to generation through verse and song.

ARABIC INFLUENCE ON THE SPANISH LANGUAGE

Given the Moorish occupation of Spain for 750 years, it is no wonder so many Arabic words and Arabic-derived phrases have been absorbed into the Spanish language—there are at least 4,000. Words beginning with "al," for instance, come from Arabic: *alabastro* ("a-la-BAS-tro")—alabaster; *albañal* ("al-ban-YAL")—sewer; *alejar* ("al-lay-HAR")—to distance or repel; and many others. As the Moors were well advanced in the study of medicine, science, and astronomy, they left a legacy of such terms, many of which have traveled to other languages, such as English and French, through Spanish. Words like algebra, alcohol, chemistry, nadir, zenith, alkaline, and cipher are examples in English.

A common expression in Spain, *Ojalá!* ("o-ha-LAH"), which means "I hope that" or "so it may come to pass," probably comes from the Muslim war cry *Wa Allah* ("WAH AHL-lah"). Similarly, the expression, *Si Dios quiere* ("see DEE-ohs kee-AY-ruh"), God willing, or if God wants to, is similar to the Arabic expression, *Insha Allah* ("EN-shah AHL-lah")—if it is the will of God.

The Moors have also lent their language to the names of many cities and towns. Generally, all those that begin with "al" were designated by the Moors during their occupation, for example, Almería, Albarracín, and Alicante.

Arabic lettering decorates the Mezquita in Córdoba. Besides language, Moorish influence is also felt in Spanish architecture and design.

SPANISH NAMES

Traditional Spanish names reflect the importance of family within Spanish culture.

It is customary for a Spanish woman to retain her maiden name after marriage. For instance, if Eva Peña marries Emilio Martínez, she becomes Señora Eva Peña de Martínez. The *de* ("day") means, in a literal sense, that Eva is "of" her husband, or the property of her husband. If Eva and Emilio have children, their last name would be Martínez-Peña. In the next generation, the mother's maiden name is dropped, unless it is a famous one. In correspondence, both names (Sr. Martínez-Peña) are used, but in conversation, only the surname (Sr. Martínez) is used.

It is also customary to name the firstborn son after the father. For instance, Emilio Martínez's son would also be called Emilio Martínez, although in conversation, especially with close relatives and friends, the son's name would include a diminutive—Emilito, which means little Emilio. The practice is also extended to female children, although it is not as common. If Eva had a daughter she named Eva, the daughter would be called Evita by family and friends. *Ita* ("EE-tah") is a suffix for "little one."

NONVERBAL FORMS OF COMMUNICATION

Spaniards, being an expressive and emotional people, use gestures along with, and as a substitute for, spoken words. Certain obviously insulting gestures, generally understood as insulting in most countries, also apply in Spain.

Flicking the teeth with the thumbnail in the direction of the second party, wiggling fingers from the nose, and grabbing the left arm with the right while making a left-handed fist are all thought to be offensive and are commonly avoided except in the most aggressive of situations. The "OK" sign, holding the thumb and forefinger to make a circle, which is a positive gesture in most countries, carries a vulgar meaning in Spain.

Other gestures express emotion or convey messages in Spain. Tapping the left elbow with the right hand is a sign that someone is a penny-pincher. Pulling down the lower eyelid while someone is talking means that the listener doubts what the speaker is saying. Making a repeated

THE CASTILIAN LISP

There is one very unusual and interesting characteristic of the Castilian language and those who speak it. In central Spain, and a few points north, a distinct lisp ("th" sound) is pronounced with the letters "S," "C" (soft "C," when followed by vowels "e" or "i"), and "Z." For instance, *Gracias* ("grah-SEE-uhs," thank you) would be pronounced "grah-THEE-uhs;" and Saragossa, Aragón's capital, would be pronounced "Thar-ah-GO-sa." In all other areas of Spain, the soft "C" and "Z" are pronounced as "S." It is interesting to note that as Castilian is generally thought of as "high Spanish," the most prestigious form, the lisp is often practiced in areas where it generally would not apply. Many Spanish speakers in Latin American countries also practice the lisp, as many of the first colonists from Spain brought it with them.

There are many theories as to how and why the Castilian lisp came into being. The most frequent explanation is that a certain Castilian king spoke with a lisp, and his courtiers, in their obsessive desire to be like the king, imitated and later adopted it. Another theory is that the lisp developed from the language of the early Greek settlers in Spain, as modern Greek pronunciation retains the lisp for certain letters. Still another maintains that the lisp developed from Arabic speech and found its way into the Spanish language during the course of the Moors' 750-year stay.

clicking noise by holding the thumb and second finger together and snapping the wrist rapidly means excitement or appreciation.

Spaniards are quick to show affection, and it is perfectly natural for all men and women to embrace upon meeting. Women will often kiss each other on the cheek, and men often walk arm-in-arm. However, the same rules of familiarity do not apply between strangers.

Eye contact between a man and a woman who are not introduced can carry a meaning of romantic interest. A woman who returns a man's gaze is interpreted as available. Similarly, it is common for men to call out expressions of appreciation to a woman as she passes on the street. As bothersome as they may be, they are said to mean no harm, and Spanish women generally do not acknowledge them.

ARTS

THE SPANISH ARE an artistic people by nature, and they put a great deal of value in creativity and self-expression. There are many cultural institutions throughout the country, one in each of the provincial capitals, and they are all overseen by the ministry of culture.

The cultural center of Spain is Madrid, although Barcelona and other large urban centers patronize the arts as well. Madrid plays host to large arts festivals during four seasons every year and also offers cultural attractions at all other times. The massive Auditorio Nacional is the capital's most important concert hall for classical music; the Teatro Real offers a variety of entertainment, including classical concerts and opera; and the Teatro de la Zarzuela is famous for its ever-changing program of ballet, concerts, opera, and traditional Spanish operetta, called *zarzuela* ("zar-zoo-EH-lah"). The Centro de Arte Reina Sofia (Queen Sofia Art Center), a museum of contemporary art, promises to be one of the most vital centers for contemporary art worldwide. It played host to the 10th anniversary of Spain's contemporary art fair (ARCO), which attracted the world's top dealers.

The most famous museum in Madrid is the Prado, which is also one of the greatest museums in the world. A veritable paradise for art lovers, the Prado houses such extraordinary works as those by Velázquez, Goya, El Greco, Rubens, Titian, and Bosch.

Opposite: **Joan Miró's work in the modern district of La Défense in Paris, France. Together with Salvador Dalí and Pablo Picasso, Joan Miró represented the modern group of Catalan artists who broke away from the conventional.**

Below: **Advertisement of a Joan Miró exhibition in a street in Barcelona.**

A room in El Greco's house. Besides being a master of Spanish painting, El Greco was also a sculptor and an architect—testimony to the full genius of the man.

Barcelona is not without its own cultural attractions, and most of them are music oriented, as Catalans are music lovers. The Gran Teatro del Liceu is respected as one of the world's greatest opera houses; the Palau de la Musica is the city's main concert hall; and every year in September, the International Music Festival draws quite a crowd to Barcelona.

EARLY MASTERS

Spain's Golden Age in art, architecture, literature, and music was the 16th and early part of the 17th century.

PAINTING Among the artists, the leading figures were Francisco de Zurbarán (1598–1664), Diego Rodriguez de Silva y Velázquez (1599–1660), Bartolomé Esteban Murillo (1617–1682), and Domenikos Theotokopoulos (1541–1614)—a Greek from the island of Crete who settled in Toledo when he was in his 30s and spent the rest of his life there. "El Greco," as he was called by the Spanish and is referred to today, typifies Spain's Golden Age like no other, even though he was not a native Spaniard. He is known for his haunting images of biblical and religious themes and his striking paintings of Toledo.

For hundreds of years, the most highly regarded of all Spanish painters was Velázquez. He was born to a well-to-do family from Seville, and his early years were filled with art lessons. He became a court painter for King Philip IV in 1623. One of Velázquez's greatest works is a portrait of Pope Innocent X. Toward the end of his life, the artist painted his masterpiece, *Las Meninas* (*The Maids of Honor*), an example of technical perfection for future generations of artists.

Murillo, like Velázquez, was born in Seville. He had virtually no formal training but displayed a great amount of innate talent. He was revered in his day for his religious paintings, most notably of the Immaculate Conception, and his paintings of street urchins and peasants. Another of Spain's great artists, Zurbarán, was born in Extremadura. That region, with its treeless plains and sunbaked landscapes, is mirrored in the powerful and austere paintings by the artist. His most renowned works, a series of religious paintings, are installed at the monastery of Guadelupe in Extremadura. The only recorded woman painter of this period is Josefa D'Obidos (1630–1684). Born in Seville, she lived most of her life in Portugal and did her best work in still life painting.

Francisco Goya y Lucientes (1746–1828) was not an artist of the Golden Age, as he lived later, but his paintings and etchings stand out as among the best in the world. He was a court painter during Charles IV's reign. Goya's later works dealt with violence, political uprisings, religious allegories, and supernatural beings.

Goya's statue in Fuende-todos, his birthplace.

Many of Goya's paintings, such as *The Witches' Sabbath,* had a nightmarish quality, and his paintings of the *Maja* ("MA-ha")—both naked and clothed—caused quite a stir. The artist's unique personal vision, combined with his artistic brilliance, made him one of the most important social commentators of his time. His etchings and drawings of the bullfight and his black-and-white series entitled *Caprichos* reflected the vices of his day.

ARCHITECTURE The greatest architects of the Golden Age were Juan de Herrera (1530–1597) and José Churriguera (1650–1723). Herrera was the principal architect of King Philip II's massive, granite palace-monastery, and his works came to typify Spanish Renaissance style. "El Escorial," as the palace is called, was begun in 1563 and completed in 1584. It made a great impression in its day but is not favored today as an architectural masterpiece because of its austerity and gloominess. However, the building is one of the most visited in Spain, for its attractions are many. Aside from being the historical home of Philip II, El Escorial contains a beautiful library with more than 40,000 rare manuscripts and ancient books, including the diaries of St. Theresa of Ávila. The museum on the property houses works by great masters such as Velázquez, El Greco, Tintoretto, and Rubens, while the church contains priceless frescoes. But perhaps the most fascinating feature of El Escorial is the Royal Pantheon, which contains the tomb of almost every Spanish king since Charles I.

The architectural works of Churriguera are much more elaborate than those of his predecessor Herrera. The best example of his Spanish baroque style is the main altar of San Esteban in Salamanca outside of Madrid.

LITERATURE The greatest literary figures of Spain's cultural Golden Age were novelist Miguel de Cervantes y Saavedra (1547–1616) and dramatists Lope Feliz de Vega Carpio (1562–1635) and Pedro Calderón de la Barca (1600–1681). Cervantes, the author of the immortal, world-famous *Don Quixote,* was born in Alcalá de Henares, east of Madrid, and his house is now a museum. In writing *Don Quixote*, the tale about the idealist and dreamer knight whose madness led him to "right all wrongs," Cervantes not only created a glorious work of fiction, but a national hero as well. Don Quixote has come to symbolize the whole heroic pattern of Spanish life and Spanish honor, as a man who committed his whole being without regard to danger. In keeping with the Spanish character, human dignity and innate goodness lead to immortality.

Statues of Don Quixote and Sancho Panza, two of the best known characters in Spanish literature, stand in front of the monument to Cervantes in the Plaza de España, Madrid.

Dramatist and poet Lope de Vega was a lyrical genius whose great body of work revolutionized theater in his day and for years to come. Cervantes himself said the man was a "prodigy of nature." He was a devout Catholic, and many of his plays take on a religious theme. The plays *Peribañez and the Comendador of Ocana* and *Fuente Ovejuna* are two of his best and most renowned. Lope de Vega took great inspiration from *The Celestina,* a story of love, lust, and moral retribution written in 1499 by Fernando de Rojas, a Jewish convert to Catholicism. Calderón de la Barca is best known for his works *The Mayor of Zalamea* and *Life Is A Dream.* His plays have a religious and philosophical theme, and like Lope, Calderón spent his later years as a priest.

The greatest poet of the Golden Age was Luis de Góngora y Argote (1561–1627), who gave his name to the poetic style called *gongorismo* ("GON-go-REES-moh"), an embellished, wordy, fantastical style of verse. Góngora's most celebrated piece of work is *Solitudes,* written in 1613.

MUSIC The regional diversity of Spain is strongly reflected in its music. Spain has produced many important composers, the art form having flourished during the reign of Isabella and Ferdinand. Juan del Encina was the leading composer of this period and a favorite of Prince Juan, the only son of the Catholic Kings. Antonio de Cabezón (1510–1566), called the Spanish Bach, was renowned for his organ music, and Cristóbal de Morales (*c.*1500–1553) for his church music. Tomás Luis de Victoria (1549–1611), a master of vocal melodies, is most famous for his *Requiem Mass,* written in 1605. Perhaps the most significant record of Spanish folk music is found in the *Cancionero de Palacio* (*Palace Song Book*), a collection of 500 or more varied musical compositions from the 15th and 16th centuries, 75 of them written by Juan del Encina.

20TH CENTURY ARTISTS

After Spain's Golden Age, artistic achievement in the 18th and 19th centuries was lacking in vitality and imagination. The 20th century, however, broke new ground, and this was especially so with architecture. Antoni Gaudí (1852–1926) was one of the most imaginative architects the world has ever seen. His style was decorative, ornate, bordering on the fantastical, and he endowed his native Barcelona with many of his works.

The most impressive of these is the Temple Expiatiori de la Sagrada Familia (Church of the Holy Family), begun in 1882 and still not completed, mostly because modern-day architects do not understand Gaudí's plans. Tragically, Gaudí was killed by a streetcar. His funeral procession was as elaborate as any great leader's, testimony to his popularity in his beloved country. His body is buried in the crypt of the Sagrada Familia.

Spanish artists wielded an incredible amount of influence on 20th century art movements. Perhaps no one was more influential than Pablo Picasso (1881–1973), the most productive artist of this or any century. Born in Málaga, Picasso emigrated to France to escape fascist sentiments in Spain at the time. He was one of the founders of Cubism, an artistic movement concerned with abstract and geometric representation of forms.

Picasso's *Guernica,* exhibited in the Prado Museum, depicts the horrors of war.

Picasso's personal vision revolutionized all forms of art: from sculpture to pottery, drawing and painting, as he was proficient in all. One of his most famous paintings is *Guernica,* a huge painting depicting the horrors of Spain's Civil War, specifically the bombing of the Basque town of Guernica by Italian and Nazi fascists. Picasso refused to let the painting enter Spain while Franco was still alive. Now, it hangs behind layers of bulletproof glass in the Prado Museum.

Other important painters include Juan Gris (1887–1927), also a cubist who emigrated to France; Joan Miró (1893–1983), a Barcelona native known for his bold, expressive images; and Salvador Dalí (1904–1989), a surrealist painter, who, like Picasso and Gris, spent much of his creative life outside of Spain. Dalí's art deserves special mention because of its fantastical subject matter: expressions of images and emotions of the artist's productive subconscious. Dalí was a great friend and sometime collaborator of Spanish filmmaker Luis Buñuel (1900–1983), who spent much of his life in Mexico. Buñuel's unique, creative approach to filmmaking influenced many.

Changes in expression by the turn of the century were also felt in literary works. A group of brilliant writers and poets, who called themselves the "Generation of 1898," produced some of the finest literature in Spain. The "Generation of 1898" was the embodiment of the new growing feelings, especially among intellectuals, of the emerging Spain. Through their writings, they sought to reveal the true soul of their beloved country. These writers expressed love of the countryside and the importance of human will and action. Above all, they advocated the Europeanization of Spain.

The most important of these writers were philosophers Miguel de Unamuno (1864–1936) and José Ortega y Gasset (1883–1955), novelist Pio Baroja (1872–1956), and poets Antonio Machado (1875–1939) and Juan Ramón Jiménez (1881–1958), who won the Nobel Prize for his poetry in 1956. Federico García Lorca (1898–1936) was another important literary figure. A supporter of the Republic at the onset of the Civil War, he was murdered by Franco's fascists. As a poet, he was instrumental in bringing new influences into the genre, and his purity of expression brought him fame beyond Spain. Most of his works have been translated into several languages.

TODAY'S MASTERS

Spain continues to produce artists of extraordinary talent. Testimony to Spain's strong musical tradition, Plácido Domingo, world renowned operatic tenor, has quite a following all over the globe, but especially in the United States, as do Montserrat Caballé and Victoria de los Angeles, famous sopranos. Pianist Alicia de Larrocha is one of the finest in the world; and before his death in 1973, Pablo Casals was lauded as the best cellist of this era. Few have been able to match the virtuosity of Andrés Segovia, the late classical guitarist.

Federico García Lorca, one of Spain's most renowned young poets, died tragically. Two of his celebrated works are *Gypsy Ballads,* written in 1928, and *Blood Wedding,* written in 1933.

Spain's contemporary art scene has dealers worldwide scrambling to represent emerging art stars Guillermo Paneque, Miquel Barcelo, and Susana Solano. Filmmakers Pedro Almodóvar and Carlos Saura have succeeded Buñuel with their talent and worldwide recognition, and writer Camilo José Cela was awarded the Nobel Prize for literature in 1989. Spain may yet experience another cultural Golden Age.

THE SPANISH GUITAR

The most characteristic instrument of Spain is the Spanish guitar. Derived from the Roman cithara, which was brought into Spain around the time of Christ, the Spanish guitar went through many forms before it evolved into the instrument we recognize today. Moorish musicians used a type of guitar that was rounded, resembling a lute. By the 16th century, all kinds of guitars were being made and used, some with as few as four and as many as seven strings, and with necks of varying sizes. By this time the instrument had come to resemble a very large fiddle, and was commonly called *vihuela de mano* ("vee-HWAY-lah day MAHN-oh") or "fiddle played by hand." The six-string guitar, with large sound box and long-fretted neck, eventually became the most popular, and this is the kind used today. The guitar suits the Spaniards well, for its integrity, potential for dreamy or impassioned sounds, and rapid rhythms.

FLAMENCO

The ultimate artistic creation of Spain is, undoubtedly, flamenco, an improvised expressive dance originating in Andalusia, and renowned and copied worldwide. But to do correct flamenco is quite difficult, and the art form takes years of instruction and practice. Flamenco has three elements: song, guitar, and dance—produced by combining supple arm and hand movements with complex heelwork. True flamenco never uses castanets (a small instrument made of wooden or ivory shells, held in the hand and clapped together to accompany dancing movements), as is often thought. Flamenco can be joyous, passionate, or very sad.

How the flamenco began in Andalusia remains a mystery, and many theories abound. Probably the most accepted one is that flamenco is Indian in origin, brought to Spain by the gypsies, who later settled in Andalusia. The early gypsies were often referred to as "flamencos," meaning either Flemish—possibly because their bright costumes resembled those of Flanders—or flamingo, so-called because, as they danced, the men gave the appearance of a flamingo, brightly colored and balanced on one leg.

Flamenco has many singing styles, but the two main ones are called *cante chico* ("KAHN-tay CHEE-koh"), meaning small song, and *cante jondo* ("KAHN-tay HON-doh"), which means deep song. A *cante chico* is lightweight and cheerful, and *cante jondo,* the more important of the two, passionate and sad. *Jaleo* ("hah-LAY-o") also accompanies flamenco, an important element of stamping feet, intricate handclapping, and the occasional, exactly placed shout of "Olé!"

A shop selling ceramics in Toledo features wares with charming folk designs. Each region has its own distinctive type of ceramics that reflects its heritage.

CRAFTS AND FOLK ART

Crafts have a long tradition in Spain, and many regions specialize in certain items. Ceramics, however, are found just about everywhere in Spain. There is usually one school devoted to the craft in every Spanish region. Influences range from Moorish to Portuguese to baroque, and techniques are handed down from generation to generation. One main center for ceramics is in Galicia, which is famous for blue and white pieces with bold decorations. The unglazed pottery of Cartagena and Aracena shows Arab influence, with the use of certain decorative motifs. The glazed pottery from Trigueros and La Palma de Condado is basically Portuguese influenced, with predominant shades of blue, green, and white. Southern Catalonia is another major area for ceramics, known for their elaborate decoration.

Leather craft is also widespread in Spain. *Botas* ("BO-tuhs"), leather wineskins, are the most popular. Handmade shoes are also quite popular in Alicante and the Balearic Islands.

Andalusia is famous for its wicker work and basketry made of both cane and olive branches. The region's fine embossed leather crafts and filigree silver are creative remnants of the Moors, as are the fine brass and copperware, marquetry (crafts using inlay of wood, ivory, or mother-of-pearl), and woven handicrafts of the area. Of course, Andalusia also specializes in handmade musical instruments, most notably the Spanish guitar.

The Balearic Islands have a long tradition of producing beautiful glass, using methods handed down quite possibly from the Moors. The tradition of iron work in Spain is especially deep rooted, and there are many schools throughout the country devoted to keeping this particularly Castilian art alive.

A damascene crafts-worker uses a small hammer to create beautiful designs for swords, plates, and various other objects. Toledo is famous for its inlaid gold work and for its damascene steel.

LEISURE

THE SPANIARDS ARE a gregarious people, filled with energy and the joy of living. This is reflected in the way they enjoy activities and leisure time. Spaniards spend their leisure time the way most Europeans do— sharing activities with family, socializing with friends, or taking in sports and other spectacles—and Spaniards do it with *gusto* ("GOO-sto"), terrific pleasure.

The family is the main social unit of Spanish life, and families truly enjoy spending time together. Weekends are spent with the family as, during the busy work week, parents and children have limited time together. A typical Saturday may include games or playtime in a nearby park, or a little promenade. Sundays are more of the same. If a family is religious, its members attend church or other places of worship together. A family may also perhaps visit relatives, attend a specified activity, or simply relax at home. A particularly well-to-do family may retreat to a weekend home, perhaps in the country, during the more temperate months. Children are much adored, and they accompany their parents everywhere.

It is not uncommon to see them at bars and restaurants until the wee hours of the morning, as their parents socialize with friends and relatives.

The Spaniard enjoys his or her siesta—that glorious, well-deserved part of the day after lunch, between 1:30 p.m. and 4 p.m., when all business stops and one takes time to enjoy the quieter side of life. Nearly everyone in Spain observes this ritual, with an afternoon stroll, the traditional nap, or a cup of coffee or glass of wine at a nearby café with friends.

Blessed with the gift of stimulating conversation, and the ability to dance, eat, and drink until dawn, the typical Spaniard is a social butterfly. Nightlife is a major activity in Spain, especially in the larger cities, and it would seem that these Spaniards never sleep. They rarely entertain at home, preferring to do so in restaurants or *tapas* ("TAH-pahs") bars, where most evenings begin. After that, they go dancing at a local club. The plazas are crowded as small groups of friends are joined by others, and conversations range anywhere from politics (Spaniards of all ages are politically versed) to fashion and American trends and movies.

Posters of a bullfight and soccer compete for attention. Soccer is Spain's most popular spectator sport, and professional clubs, such as Real Madrid, have ardent fans who follow them wherever they play.

SOCCER—THE FAVORITE SPORT

The Spaniards love sports, and soccer is the number one favorite. There are many amateur soccer teams and stadiums all over the country, but the best and most important are in Madrid and Barcelona.

The most popular is Real Madrid, which plays in Madrid's Santiago Bernabeu Stadium, a huge arena holding 130,000 spectators. Real Madrid won the UEFA Cup title in 1985 and 1986. The Atlético Madrid team is based just outside the city, and its home base is the Vicente Calderón Stadium. The soccer team of Barcelona won the European Cup in 1989.

Most Spaniards would prefer to see a soccer game in person, but with television sets in just about every home and bar, those who cannot get to the stadium still enjoy the game. Soccer players become veritable celebrities in Spain, gross hefty salaries, and are the heroes of young boys.

OTHER SPORTS

Golf, tennis, sailing, and other water sports are also popular with Spaniards and are well suited to the climate. Sailing in particular is a favorite of King Juan Carlos I, who keeps his own fleet of sailboats on Majorca in the Balearic Islands. Golf is another main attraction, and there are excellent courses, especially in the southern regions and along the Mediterranean. Many professional players have attained international fame, most notably Severiano Ballasteros. Tennis is more of a spectator sport than anything else in Spain, but its fans are loyal. Several tennis clubs throughout the country host international championships to packed grandstands.

Cycling, too, is a sport gaining wide popularity, especially since Spaniards Pedro Delgado and Miguel Indurain won the Tour de France in 1988 and 1991, respectively. Spain also has a Tour de España bicycle race. Madrid each year hosts an annual bicycle day. Roads are closed off, and many riders, in varying states of fitness, take to the bicycle.

Snow-skiing is another popular pastime in Spain. With so many mountain ranges, it is possible for Spaniards to ski at various points all over the country, and in all kinds of weather. A snowy slope is often just a few hours' drive from a sunny beach.

As Spain has so many miles of coastline, wind-surfing, swimming, or simply sunbathing on one of the many crowded beaches are popular activities.

The six major areas for skiing in Spain are the Cantabrian Mountains, the Catalan Pyrénées, the Aragónese Pyrénées, El Sistema Ibérico, the most easterly mountain range, El Sistema Central, close to Madrid in the center of the country, and El Sistema Penibético, the southernmost mountain chain, in the heart of the Sierra Nevada.

TRADITIONAL ATTRACTIONS

The Basque national sport is pelota, an extremely fast court game also popular in Latin America and parts of the United States. The Basque word for pelota is *jai alai* ("HI uh-LIE"), which means "joyous festival" in their language. It is also known as jai alai in other parts of the world. Jai alai developed from an ancient sport, originally a rural game that simply involved hitting a ball against a wall with one's hand.

Today's jai alai is more complex and infinitely more dangerous. Players propel a rock-hard ball against a wall with a long-shaped basket strapped to the wrist, but the type of wall and the size of basket vary according to difficulty and type of match. The most common wall is the three-sided *fronton* ("fron-TOHN") and the least common, four-sided or *trinquete* ("treen-kee-EH-teh"). Walls may be long, short, or slope-roofed. Similarly, the baskets the players wear can be single-handed or double-handed, rubber- or leather-lined, longer or shorter. Spectators bet on the outcome of the match, and it takes a real knowledge of the game to bet well. Unfortunately, the finest players in Spain usually do not stay, but depart for the United States, especially Miami, Florida, to seek stardom there.

Pelota—one of the fastest and most strenuous games in the world—is played in a walled concrete court.

BULLFIGHTING

To say bullfighting is a mere sport would surely be an injustice. In Spain, a bullfight is a spectacle, a ceremony, a drama; the veritable heart and soul of the country and the people. In fact, the Spanish language does not even use the word "fight" in describing the much-loved event: rather *corrida de toros* ("koh-REE-dah day TOH-ros"), which means "running, or fiesta, of the bulls," a much more dignified term. Bullrings are found all over Spain, but the most important are in Madrid and Seville. Indeed, there are even museums dedicated to the sport, and many writers and artists have been inspired by the ceremony of the spectacle. American writer Ernest Hemingway immortalized the pageantry and danger of the bullfight in two books, *The Sun Also Rises* and *Death in the Afternoon*.

Portrait of a bullfighter at the Bullfight Museum, Córdoba.

The origins of bullfighting can be traced back to the Bronze Age in Crete, when young boys tested their worth by throwing themselves onto the horns of pasturing bulls. During Spain's early Christian age, the pastime was outlawed, but then it was restored again by the Moors during their occupation. Since then, bullfighting has always had a strong following in Spain, if not by the ruling kings and queens, at least by the general population. Interestingly enough, in earlier years, the bullfights were fought by nobles to impress their peers, lady friends, and subjects, and only on horseback. This changed in the 17th century, when paid fighters from the lower classes took over and transformed the event in many ways. Commoner Francisco Romero, in 1725, is credited as being the first man to have killed a bull on foot, to the delight of the crowd. The first bullring was erected in Madrid much later, in 1743.

The matador and his team.

Banderillero

Picador

As with other rituals, the bullfight is complex. It always begins with a parade and ceremony. The focal point is the matador, who has assistants called *banderilleros* ("bahn-deh-ree-YAY-ros," or those on foot) and *picadores* ("pee-kuh-DOR-rays," or those on horseback). The assistants enter the ring with the matador and proceed to taunt the animal by waving brightly colored capes and jabbing it with long dart sticks. This helps to enrage the bull and also gives the matador the chance to observe the bull in action and to gauge its temperament. Next comes the finale, as the matador, dressed in his bejeweled suit (referred to as a "suit of lights"), begins a series of intricate maneuvers with cape and sword, working quite close to the bull. The tension builds until the exact moment when the matador aims for the spot between the bull's shoulders, and plunges his sword in. The crowd customarily cheers

Opposite: **In Spain, bull-fighting is not just a sport but an art that is ancient and traditional, reflecting the psyche of a country and its people.**

wildly, *Olé!*, and throws flowers into the ring. But Spanish crowds are hard to please. Even if the matador succeeds in killing and not being killed, unless he fought well and with dignity, he does not get the favor of the crowd. A Spaniard knows his bullfight.

Successful matadors have become wealthy in Spain. Some of the more famous ones of this century are Manolete, who was killed tragically in the bullring in 1947, Juan Belmonte, Luis Dominguín, Antonio Ordoñez, and Manuel Benítez, known as El Cordobés.

A FLURRY OF ACTIVITY

The year 1992 was an important year for Spain. Spaniards, always content to be enthusiastic spectators, were participants of a sort as Barcelona hosted the summer Olympics and Seville the Expo '92 Universal Exhibition. Madrid was designated the "Cultural Capital of Europe" for 1992. To prepare for the 1992 Summer Olympic Games, Barcelona underwent major renovations. Entire city blocks in unkempt neighborhoods were spruced up or even razed. The main stadiums, which can hold hundreds of thousands of people, were built in the Montjuïc area. And, along the sea front, a mini city was erected to house the 20,000 athletes, trainers, and officials involved in the games. In Madrid, a program of restoration was undertaken to transform the Plaza Mayor and its environs. An outdoor sculpture museum, two new theaters, and a new design center were also added to the building program. Like Barcelona and Madrid, Seville also made great efforts to spruce up the city. Roads and airports were improved, new hotels built, and old buildings restored, such as Seville's magnificent Gothic cathedral.

In addition, all over Spain there were celebrations to mark the 500th anniversary of Columbus' voyage to America and to celebrate the contribution of Jewish and Arab cultures to Spain. The country received over 10 million visitors for these events. After the isolation of the Franco years, and the difficult transition to democracy, it was easy to see why the Spaniards were so excited. Spain was participating once again in the mainstream of European—even world—culture.

FESTIVALS

SPANIARDS TAKE TO FESTIVALS like few other people in the world. A happy, lively people, they are truly at ease in their celebrations and plan all year for them. Spanish celebrations, whose origins go back hundreds, even thousands of years, are steeped in tradition, folklore, history, and regional pride. There are hundreds of festivals, each one a testimony to Spanish creativity. Fiestas and religious celebrations, both somber and joyous, are observed in accordance with the Christian calendar, the most important ones being Holy Week and Corpus Christi. There are *ferias* ("feh-REE-uhs"), popular fairs held in every town and village of Spain. Seville's April Fair is renowned for its colorful horseback processions and full range of activities.

There are festivals on the occasion of a grape harvest or the selling of livestock. There are those that signify a particular moment in history or that herald the beginning of spring, summer, fall, or winter. And each and every town in Spain, no matter how large or small, honors its patron saint with the requisite feasting, parades, and floats. Appropriately, flamenco dancing, music, and bullfights are the highlight of all fiestas.

Festivals are a time for traditional dress and Old World ways. All the townspeople gather on the streets and in the main square and proceed on a carpet of confetti and flowers. The children especially are a sight to behold in their full traditional regalia. Girls have their hair tied back, with a colorful bloom at the nape of their neck, wearing beads and carrying baskets of flowers. Boys wear *boleros* ("boh-LAY-rohs," short, slim-fitting jackets), cummerbunds, and hats.

Opposite: **A young dancer with a lute prepares to join in a festival in La Mancha.**

Below: **Central to Spanish life are fiestas. During such occasions, streets are festooned with banners.**

Opposite: Valencia is fa-
mous for an unusual
event, Las Fallas of San
José. During the week-
long feast, huge figures
of wood, papier-mâché,
and cloth are erected by
competing teams in the
main plazas.

CARNIVAL

Carnival is celebrated all over Spain, symbolizing the final abandonment before Lent, the season of penitence in the Catholic Church. All over the country there is much display of gaiety, music, decoration, and color, with parades and dancing in the streets. Daily activities halt as tourists and Spaniards alike rejoice in the annual festival. Cádiz and the island of Tenerife have some of the most spectacular celebrations.

LAS FALLAS

This end-of-winter celebration in Valencia is a week-long fiesta to honor Valencia's patron saint, San José (Saint Joseph, father of Jesus and patron saint of carpenters). According to legend, in the Middle Ages, the Brotherhood of Carpenters burned accumulated wood shavings on March 19, St. Joseph's Day. Today, more elaborate activities take place. All usual daily duties cease from March 12 to 19. Huge figures, often satirical versions of historical and contemporary persons, are erected in all the main plazas. There is feasting, music, dancing, and the first bullfights of the season. Prizes are awarded for the best *paella* ("pie-EL-ah," a rice-based dish), figure design, fireworks, and flower display. In a great show of drama, as in the Middle Ages, everything is burned to ashes in collective bonfires the night of the 19th.

ROMERÍAS

Festivities surrounding *romerías* ("roh-meh-REE-uhs"), or pilgrimages, in Spain mark the journeys of the faithful to specific shrines or sanctuaries. Always accompanied by fanfare of some kind, the festivities begin on the first day of the pilgrimage and end on the saint's day they commemorate.

Undoubtedly, the most popular *romería* in Spain is that of Andalusia's El Rocío, also marking the end of spring. In the province of Huelva along the Costa de la Luz, in a typical Andalusian procession, people on horseback and in flower-covered wagons and carriages from all over Spain converge to make their way to the shrine of the Virgin of El Rocío in Almonte. As is the custom, many days are devoted to mass, offerings, and prayers, accompanied by song, dance, and wine-drinking. At dawn on the final day, the Virgin is removed from her shrine and paraded through the crowd.

SEMANA SANTA: HOLY WEEK

Semana Santa, or Holy Week, a week-long celebration commemorating the passion of Jesus Christ, is celebrated in Spain like nowhere else. It is said that only the Spaniards have a gift for reliving the passion so ardently.

The manifestation of Holy Week festivities has no set of written rules, yet the activities beginning the week before Easter are quite similar in all areas of Spain. The Holy Week celebration is deeply rooted, ancient, and picturesque. It can also be among the most disturbing, as the processions can take on an almost frightening air. Massive floats carrying the figures of Christ, the Virgin, and depictions of Christ's Passion (the sufferings of Christ on the cross) are carried by costumed penitents chosen from among the people. Before them, and accompanied by drum rolls and the clanking of chains on the pavement, hundreds of robed and hooded penitents walk through the streets to atone for the sins of the past year.

Without a doubt, Holy Week celebrations in Seville are the most important and original. Thousands of local citizens and tourists line the streets day and night as the elaborate figures and floats make their way

A Holy Week procession in Málaga. One of the most dramatic religious events of the year, Holy Week is celebrated passionately all over Spain.

through. All converge on Seville's extraordinary Gothic cathedral. But there are other important Holy Week celebrations as well. In Lorca in the region of Murcia, the townspeople exhibit great imagination as biblical characters are represented by the villagers wearing masks. Valladolid, the capital of Castile-León, is famous for its magnificent but quite solemn interpretation of Holy Week, featuring beautiful baroque sculpture and religious figures chosen from their museum, which houses the finest religious icons and statues in the country.

Fiesta of the Three Kings is a favorite festival among the young.

EPIPHANY

January 6, the day of the Epiphany, is also the day of gift-giving in Spain. On this day, many towns hold parades for the Three Kings. Floats and figures make their way through streets and plazas, and candles are thrown to children along the route.

On the fifth, the eve of Epiphany, in anticipation of gifts galore, children put their shoes out on porches and balconies. They awake the next morning to find presents inside their shoes, left by the Three Kings.

NEW YEAR'S EVE

New Year's Eve is a family celebration in Spain. At midnight, all members of the family eat one grape for each stroke of the clock and drink champagne.

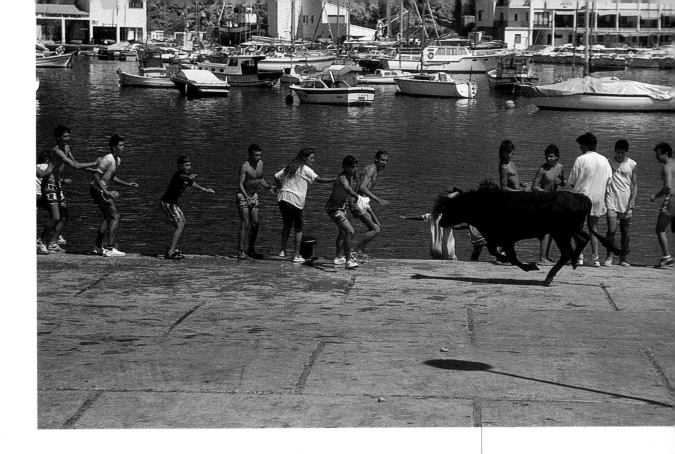

SAN FERMIN: THE RUNNING OF THE BULLS

Every summer, from July 6 to 14, Pamplona celebrates the beginning of its bullfighting season with a week's worth of activities, wine, and gaiety. Immortalized by Ernest Hemingway in *The Sun Also Rises*, the San Fermin festivities in Pamplona are among the most popular and most joyous.

Very early each morning, the bulls that are to fight in the ring in the afternoon are released into the streets, guided by barriers. Men show their courage and speed by racing ahead of the bulls through the streets to the bullring. Sometimes they are wounded or even killed. Taverns are crowded to the brim that week with brave men recounting their heroic feats.

The running of the bulls in Pamplona also makes for brave little children. Part of the festivities includes a man in costume and three-cornered hat. As children race to get out of his way, the costumed man attempts to strike them to make them behave.

Running of the bulls—a spectacle not to be missed.

FOOD

THE CUISINE OF SPAIN is as varied as the country itself. Bordering the Mediterranean Sea, the Atlantic Ocean, France, and Portugal, and having been subjected to so many invasions, conquests, and influences, Spain has produced a cuisine that is as rich in flavor as it is in history. It is an inspired combination of the very exotic and the very simple.

CULINARY INFLUENCES

The occupation of Spain by the Moors for 750 years greatly influenced the culinary development of the country. Bringing with them their own rich culinary heritage, the Moorish invaders introduced the cultivation of rice, now a staple food; spices such as saffron, cumin, and anise; nuts (especially almonds); and fruits such as figs, citrus, and bananas. The technique of marinating fish in a strong, vinegary sauce, the combinations of sweet and spicy foods, of legumes and greens, are most certainly of Arab origin.

From the conquests of the New World in the 15th century came eggplant, tomatoes, potatoes, red and green peppers, both hot and sweet, and chocolate. But Spain is not without its own indigenous culinary features. Just as the Spanish peasants in rural villages ate simple seasonal food for hundreds of years, Spaniards today still eat seasonally, relying on the simple excellence of the natural resources produced by each of the country's regions.

Opposite: **Roast chicken, a Spanish favorite, sold on a street corner in Barcelona.**

Below: **Spain is one of Europe's top agricultural countries. Here, an indoor market sells all kinds of agricultural produce from Spain's rich farmlands.**

The Mediterranean sun and climate, the lush pastures of the northwest, the Nordic temperatures of the mountain regions, and the seafood-laden coastlines combine to produce an enormous variety of excellent produce, meat, and dairy products.

A *churros* maker at work.

MEALTIMES AND TYPICAL MEALS

Spaniards are known for eating late and for not eating light. There is one exception, though—breakfast. Breakfast, usually served between 7 and 8 a.m., is simple, consisting of rolls, butter or preserves (the only meal where bread is served with butter), and coffee. Spanish coffee is a strong espresso, usually taken straight or mixed with hot milk. For the young at heart, there is also the children's favorite—*churros* ("CHOO-ros"), strips of sugared fried dough dipped in thick hot chocolate.

Lunch is the main meal of the day for the Spaniards. Served between 2 and 3 p.m., it may start with a soup, followed by a salad with a fish or meat course and perhaps some vegetables—or maybe even a hearty paella. It is becoming more common in big cities for working people to grab a sandwich at a nearby tavern or restaurant. But the norm is to eat a big meal, and to eat it leisurely. Lunch is eaten with bread, no butter, and a bottle of wine. Bottles of mineral water or tap water are served at every meal.

Dinner is eaten very late—almost never before 9 p.m. and sometimes even as late as midnight. If it is a family meal eaten at home, the meal may be light: a simple potato omelet served cold is common, or cold meats, cheeses, and bread. For a social occasion, however, the dinner may be different. An evening out with friends is usually preceded by a stop, or two, at a *tapas* bar. The evening will then begin around 7 p.m.

Tapas, an age-old custom in Spain, are found all across the country, in big cities as well as in little mountain villages and coastal resorts. It is a special feature of Spanish dining, eaten sometimes before lunch, but usually before dinner, and is more a style of eating than a particular food.

Appetizing *tapas* for a mid-afternoon break.

The types of *tapas* are as varied as the regions of Spain. They consist of sampling portions of delicacies, first or main courses, or whatever abounds. They can be as simple as marinated olives, grilled sausage, or anchovies on toast, or as elaborate as an herb-filled rice salad, marinated stuffed squid, or meatballs with saffron sauce. Each bar may have one or more specialties. Cubes of cured ham are a simple and popular favorite.

As dinner is taken so late, there is still plenty of appetite after a good round of *tapas*. Typical dinners consist of a soup, vegetables, and a light meat or fish course. Although Spaniards like to nibble on sweets, cakes, and cookies throughout the day (another legacy from the Moors), they are not really dessert lovers, and prefer a piece of fruit to top off a meal.

There is, however, a particular penchant for flan, an egg custard flavored with orange, coffee, chocolate, or caramel. And sweets, such as quince paste eaten with fresh goat cheese, or a similar cheese, are popular.

A market stall offers meat products from hams to sausages.

REGIONAL SPECIALTIES

To break down the flavors of Spain into one category would surely be a disservice. As there are so many influences, there are many regional specialties and as many ways to cook those specialties as there are cooks in Spain. To sample all the food that Spain has to offer would be a culinary journey. From the mountains to the coasts to the plains, there exist many dishes, tastes, and smells.

There are, however, a few generalities.

Spain is basically a rice-eating country, and many dishes are made with rice. They range from the very elaborate to the very simple—as when rice is baked with whatever is handy in the kitchen: a piece of bacon fat for flavor or a single piece of fish.

Just as basic in Spanish dishes is the humble egg. Egg dishes are found throughout the country, in restaurants, taverns, and at home. The potato omelet, served at room temperature or colder, is a favorite. *Huevos flamencos* ("WEH-buhs flah-MEN-kos"), fried eggs baked with ham, tomatoes, and vegetables, traditionally a dish from Seville, is now found all over Spain. But whatever the preparation, Spanish egg dishes are always savory and satisfying.

Also popular are *cocidos* ("koh-SEE-dohs"), or traditional Spanish stews. These are usually a combination of fresh and dried vegetables with different meats, and every province has its own creative version—and its own name: Catalans refer to the dish as *escudella* ("eh-scoo-DAY-yuh") and the Andalusians, *potaje* ("poh-TAH-hay"). Every province also makes great use of *chorizo* ("choh-REE-soh"), a spicy smoked sausage. Truly the essence of Spanish cooking, *chorizo* finds its way into just about every dish.

GREEN SPAIN The northwest is one of the richest areas for food. It is known for its hearty dishes that ward off the chill of the region.

The cuisine of the Basque country is famous for its pork and seafood, such as baby eels cooked in hot oil with hot chillies. Another popular dish is *bacalao* ("bah-kuh-LAH-oh") or dried salt cod. One of the most versatile foods, it can be cooked with onions and peppers, or blended into a purée with cream, olive oil, garlic, and other spices. Another interesting way to cook *bacalao* is to slowly simmer it in garlic, which produces a gelatinous sauce with the consistency of mayonnaise.

BACALAO

As in the past, *bacalao* is still considered a staple food. In Spain, as in other poor Catholic countries, Lent was strictly observed. As it was forbidden to eat meat, households had to rely on a meat substitute that could be stored for days, and one that was easily affordable.

Bacalao needs much preparation, however. Since it must be desalted before cooking, cooks first slap the fish against a hard surface to break down the fibers, and then leave it to stand under running water, or soak for at least 24 hours, changing the water frequently. Once the fish is ready to be cooked, it is never boiled, only simmered gently.

Galicia's famed *empanada*.

The Cantabrian valleys produce rich cream and butter products, used extensively in their cuisine. *Sobaos* ("soh-BAH-ohs") and *quesada pasiega* ("kay-SAH-duh pah-see-YAY-guh") are two local dessert specialties made with the excellent dairy products of this region.

Well-known dishes of Asturias are *fabada asturiana* ("fah-BAH-duh ass-too-ree-AH-nuh"), or butter beans and sausage, and *morcilla* ("mor-SEE-yuh"), thick cornbread eaten with blood sausage. The region's *picón* ("pee-KON") cheese and cider are favorites and available at just about every bar and tavern.

The isolated region of Galicia is said to have the finest cuisine in all of Spain, or at least the finest array of fish and shellfish, which the Galicians prepare well. For shellfish, the region boasts oysters, tiny clams, mussels, and shrimps. From the seas come sardines, hake, cod, and octopus, and from the freshwater rivers and streams, trout, salmon, and crayfish—to name just a few. The lamprey eel is another favorite, treasured in Spain since ancient times, and scallops, baked and stuffed, are served everywhere.

Marinated sardines done Spanish-style. Fish is an important food staple, and northern Spain is known for its fish dishes.

But Galicia is not only famous for its seafood. It is also famous for the *empanada* ("ehm-pa-NAH-duh"), a small handheld pie, double-crusted, oiled, colored with saffron, and stuffed with an array of fillings, from fish to pork to vegetables.

Although the origin of the *empanada* is unknown, it has been popular for centuries. In the medieval dining hall of Santiago's cathedral monastery, amid the other carvings, there is a carved relief of a man holding an *empanada*.

INLAND SPAIN This is the region of roasts—lamb, veal, suckling pig, kid goat, and other game. Their extraordinary taste and texture come from meticulous roasting in wood-fired and clay ovens. Inland Spain also boasts some of the best sausage and cheese products in the world.

La Rioja, a peaceful farming area with an abundance of trout streams, is known as much for its cuisine as for its wine. León also serves typical inland fare. Roast suckling pig goes well with the region's strong wines.

La Mancha is known for its good wines and is the home of Spain's favorite cheese, *manchego* ("mahn-CHAY-go") The specialty of Extremadura is its lamb stew, a savory dish boldly seasoned with paprika and recommended only for the hearty!

Madrid has no real cuisine of its own, but it does have a number of city-oriented and sweet dishes. The region's *cocido madrileño* ("koh-SEE-doh mah-dree-LAY-nyoh") is prepared throughout Spain—a stew of chickpeas, vegetables, beef, chicken, bacon, and sausage, served in three courses: the broth as the first course, followed by the vegetables, and then the meats.

A great variety of cheeses is offered in this provision store in Madrid. Many of Spain's cheeses are exported.

THE PYRÉNÉES The cuisine of this region is typically a mountain cuisine. Trout and other fish from the many mountain streams are cooked *a la llosa* ("ah lah YOH-sah")—on a slate slab over hot coals. Beef can also be prepared this way. Typical game specialties are stews featuring wild boar or mountain goat. Dishes made with rabbit, quail, partridge, venison, and duck are also popular. And wild mushrooms are a local delicacy.

MEDITERRANEAN SPAIN All over the Mediterranean region, virtually every type of seafood makes its way into a meal, from the impressive lobster to baby eels, prawns, spider crabs, and anchovies. Along the Mediterranean, dinner can be a modest yet hearty meal of a simple fish soup, a creative seafood-stuffed omelet, or a stew of shellfish and fish cooked in a rich tomato sauce.

Catalonia blends the best culinary elements of both neighboring France and Spain. Known for garlicky fried croquettes of cod and potatoes, Catalonia is also home to spicy sauces such as *romesco* ("roh-MESS-koh," a blend of peppers, hazelnuts, and olive oil) and *alioli* ("ah-lee-OH-lee," a garlic mayonnaise that dresses many dishes).

Murcia and Valencia are both famed for their rice creations, but perhaps the best loved is native to Valencia. Paella valenciana is a flavorful combination of saffron rice, seafood (clams, mussels, lobster, fish), chicken, and vegetables (peas, beans, tomatoes, pimentos).

The amounts vary, but the combinations are important: the red, green, and yellow of the dish are also the colors of Spain. Spaniards eat paella almost exclusively at midday.

SOUTHERN SPAIN The Arab influence on Spain's cuisine is perhaps most apparent in Andalusia, known for its spicy sauces, chunky pepper

Paella valenciana, a delicious rice dish from Valencia province, is one of the most well-known dishes of Spain.

relishes, and herbed marinades. *Tapas* originated here, and it is said that the best *tapas* in all of Spain can still be found in Andalusia.

Southern Spain's dishes are simply prepared: grilled onions with herbs, crusty bread, and a sharp red wine. *Gazpacho* ("gahz-PAH-choh"), a cold tomato-based soup, with cucumbers, peppers, garlic, oil, and olives, makes a whole meal as it is traditionally served with hardboiled eggs, bread, cheese, and wine. Trevelez ham is famous throughout Spain.

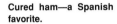
Cured ham—a Spanish favorite.

BALEARIC AND CANARY ISLANDS The cuisine of these islands is exciting and imaginative, as it must sometimes overcome the limits of supply.

Seafood is at the heart of many of the local dishes of the Balearic Islands. And both fish and meat pies are popular. A traditional dish is a type of flat pizza, brushed with oil and topped with vegetables.

Majorca boasts *sobrasada* ("soh-brah-SAH-duh") and *butifarras* ("boo-tee-FAH-ruhs"), both spicy sausages, the former spiced with red pepper, the latter with cinnamon. *Ensaimada* ("ehn-sai-MAH-duh"), a favorite dessert of light puff pastry that can vary considerably in size, is made from, among other things, pork fat. The Canary Islands have many delicious dishes based on the simple combination of fish and *mojo picón* ("MOH-hoh pee-KON"), a spicy, tart, and garlicky sauce that gives an unmistakable flavor to the islands' foods.

WINE

Wine is drunk at every meal, either straight or diluted with mineral or carbonated water or 7-Up (a favorite of teenagers). It is said that Spaniards drink more wine than any other people in the world. For thousands of years, wine has been produced on Spanish soil, beginning with the Phoenician traders in 1100 B.C. and later, the Romans in 200 B.C.

The wines of Green Spain are slightly acid and the perfect accompaniment to the seafood dishes of the area.

Galicia's Cambados and Ribeiro wines have gained international attention. The white Ribeiro, traditionally served in little porcelain cups, is quite acidic. The red Ribeiro is robust and popular. Of special interest is the *albarino* ("ahl-bey-REE-noh") wine, a white wine made from grapes introduced by monks on pilgrimages from the Rhine and Moselle valleys.

The hard cider of Asturias is popular throughout Europe.

The La Rioja region of inland Spain produces the best of Spanish table wines, prized reds and unique whites. As these wines grow in fame and popularity, there are now strict regulations governing their production and labeling to prevent fraud.

Catalonia, along the Mediterranean coast, is the home of the exceptional Catalan *cava* ("KAH-vah"), a sparkling wine whose taste and quality competes well with French champagne. It is still made in the traditional manner.

Also of note are the fortified wines and smooth brandies of Andalusia in southern Spain. From Jerez de la Frontera come the dry golden wines known abroad as sherries in honor of the town of Jerez where the first wineries were established.

The Canary Islands are home to the wines of Temerie and El Hierro, praised by Shakespeare's Falstaff.

In addition, the malmsey of La Palma and Lanzarote are also prized.

COOK A SPANISH MEAL

A recipe for Galician shellfish salad

1 lb. (500 g) shrimps	4 oz. (125 g) onion
1 lb. (500 g) medium prawns	1 clove garlic
2 lb. (1 kg) mussels	4 fluid oz. (125 ml) olive oil
1 lb. (500 g) lobster	2 teaspoons sherry vinegar
5 oz. (150 g) green pepper	salt
5 oz. (150 g) red pepper	2 hard-boiled eggs, sliced
7 oz. (200 g) tomatoes	chopped parsley

Cook and clean the shellfish. Cut them into small pieces. Then chop the vegetables and toss the prepared ingredients together. Season with oil, vinegar, and salt. Decorate with eggs and parsley.

Serve cold. This recipe serves four people.

Spaniards are sociable and enthusiastic diners.
In restaurants, a variety of dishes is usually ordered para picar *("PAH-rah pee-KAHR")— to nibble at.*

TABLE MANNERS

Spain generally follows Continental customs for table manners. Spaniards eat with the fork in the left hand and the knife in the right. The knife is used to push food onto the fork, and then the fork is raised, upside down, to the mouth. Neither fingers nor bread are used to put food onto the fork, or into the mouth. Wrists are kept on the table, and hands never rest on the lap.

At a dinner party, the guest of honor would be seated to the right of the host, while the hostess sits at the other end of the table, opposite the host. There is no pressure on those guests who do not partake of a certain food or drink. In fact, Spaniards hate to see food wasted and consider it more polite to decline extra helpings than to leave food untouched on the plate. A typical Spanish meal and get-together may last much past midnight.

Manners for eating at *tapas* bars are quite lenient. Olive pits and shells from shrimp are discarded quite naturally onto the floor.

SPAIN

A **B** **C** **D**

1

Bay of Biscay

FRANCE

Gulf of Lion

ATLANTIC OCEAN

La Coruña
Gijón
Oviedo
Santander
Bilbao
San Sebastian
Santiago
ASTURIAS *Picos de Europa* **CANTABRIA**
GALICIA
Vigo
BASQUE PROVINCES
Pamplona
ANDORRA
Pico de Aneto
Cantabrian Mts.
NAVARRE
Pyrenees

2

CASTILE-LEÓN
Duero
LA RIOJA
Ebro Saragossa
CATALONIA
Costa Brava
ARAGÓN
Salamanca
Castilian Mountains
Sierra de Guadarrama
Segovia
Ávila
Iberian Mountains
Barcelona
PORTUGAL
Sierra de Gredos
MADRID
Guadalajara
Tagus
Toledo

VALENCIA
Gulf of Valencia
EXTREMADURA
CASTILE-LA MANCHA
Valencia
BALEARIC ISLANDS
Meseta
Júcar
Majorca

3

Plateau
Ibiza
Sierra Morena
Costa Blanca
Alicante
MURCIA
Guadalquivir
Jaén
Córdoba
Torres
Cartagena
Seville
ANDALUSIA
Costa Cálida
Doñana National Park
Granada
Sierra Nevada
Mulhacén
MEDITERRANEAN SEA
Gulf of Cádiz
Málaga
Almería
4
Cádiz
Costa del Sol
Gibraltar (U.K.)
Strait of Gibraltar
Ceuta (Spain)
ALGERIA

Melilla (Spain)

● Capital city
● Major town
▲ Mountain F
■ Ancient Site

5

CANARY ISLANDS
La Palma
Lanzarote
Tenerife
Santa Cruz de Tenerife
MOROCCO
La Gomera
Mount Teide
(12,195 ft / 3,715 m)
Gran Canaria
Fuerteventura
Hierro
WESTERN SAHARA

Feet	M
16,500	5
9,900	3
6,600	2
3,300	1
1,650	
660	
0	

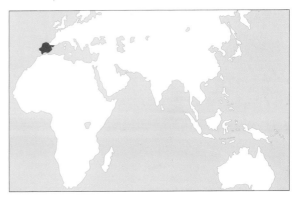

QUICK NOTES

LAND AREA
195,988 square miles (507,609 square km), including the mainland and the Balearic and Canary Islands

POPULATION
39 million

CAPITAL
Madrid

MAJOR CITIES
Barcelona, Valencia, Seville, Saragossa, Bilbao, Málaga, Córdoba, Valladolid, Murcia, Granada, Salamanca

AUTONOMOUS REGIONS
Andalusia, Aragón, Asturias, Balearic Islands, Basque Provinces, Canary Islands, Cantabria, Castile-La Mancha, Castile-León, Catalonia, Extremadura, Galicia, Madrid, Murcia, Navarre, La Rioja, Valencia

HIGHEST POINT
Mount Teide (12,195 feet or 3,715 m)

NATIONAL ANTHEM
Marcha Real Granadera ("March of the Royal Grenadier")

OFFICIAL LANGUAGE
Castilian

MAJOR REGIONAL LANGUAGES
Catalan, Galician, Basque (or Euskera)

MAJOR RELIGION
Roman Catholic

MAJOR RIVERS
Ebro, Guadalquivir, Tagus, Duero, Júcar

CURRENCY
Peseta
(US$1 = 114 pesetas)

CLIMATE
Varied: cold winters and hot dry summers in the central regions; cool and humid along the northern coast; moderate winters and hot summers in the south

MAIN EXPORTS
Grains, citrus, olives and olive oil, wine grapes, tobacco

NATIONAL LEADERS
Charles I—King of Spain, 1516–1556, during Spain's Golden Age
Francisco Franco—Dictator of Spain, 1939–1975
Juan Carlos I—King of Spain since 1975
Felipe González Márquez—Prime Minister of Spain since 1982 and leader of the Spanish Socialist Workers' Party (PSOE), the leading political party of the legislature

GLOSSARY

bachillerato ("bah-KEE-yay-RAH-toh")
Exam taken at the end of secondary school.

banderilleros ("bahn-deh-ree-YAY-ros")
Men on foot who assist the matador.

botas ("BO-tuhs")
Leather wineskins.

Chapurriao ("CHAH-poo-ree-OW")
A mixture of Castilian and Catalan languages.

conversos ("con-BER-sos")
Jews who converted to Catholicism.

corrida de toros ("koh-REE-dah day TOH-ros")
Running of the bulls, or bullfight.

Euskera ("yoo-SKAY-rah")
Basque name for the Basque language.

ferias ("feh-REE-uhs")
Fairs, generally held on festive occasions.

fronton ("fron-TOHN")
Three-sided wall used for playing pelota.

gitanos ("gee-TAH-nos")
A group of gypsies who live mostly in southern and central Spain.

gongorismo ("GON-go-REES-moh")
An embellished, wordy, fantastic poetic style.

gusto ("GOO-sto")
Great pleasure.

huerta ("WEHR-tah")
A coastal or irrigated fertile plain.

húngaros ("HOONG-gah-ros")
Nomadic gypsies from Central Europe.

jai alai ("HI-uh-LIE")
Basque word for the game of pelota.

marranos ("mah-RAH-nos")
Lapsed Jewish converts to Catholicism who secretly practiced their Jewish faith.

moriscos ("moh-REES-kos")
Moors who converted to Catholicism.

Ojalá ("o-ha-LAH")
A common Spanish expression meaning "I hope it may come to pass."

patria chica ("pah-TREE-ya CHEE-kah")
Native region.

picadores ("pee-kuh-DOR-rays")
Men on horseback who assist the matador.

rias ("REE-uhs")
Rocky inlets found along Spain's coastline.

romerías ("roh-meh-REE-uhs")
Pilgrimage to a religious shrine, with much festivity.

Si Dios quiere ("see DEE-ohs kee-AY-ruh")
Expression meaning "God willing" or "if God wants to."

tapas ("TAH-pahs")
Savory snacks sold at *tapas* bars.

toros bravos ("TOH-rohs BRAH-bos")
Bulls bred to fight in the ring.

trinquete ("treen-kee-EH-teh")
Four-sided wall used for playing pelota.

zarzuela ("zar-zoo-EH-lah")
Traditional Spanish operetta.

BIBLIOGRAPHY

Caistor, Nick. *Spain*. Austin: Steck-Vaughn, 1992.

Feinberg, Ellen Okner. *Following the Milky Way: A pilgrimage across Spain*. Ames: Iowa State University Press, 1989.

Miller, Arthur. *Spain*. New York: Chelsea House, 1989.

Solsten, Eric. *Spain, A Country Study*. Washington: U.S. Government Printing Office, 1990.

Tolhurst, Marilyn. *Spain*. Englewood Cliffs: Silver Burdett Press, 1989.

INDEX

INDEX

INDEX

PICTURE CREDITS
Life File Photo Library: 6, 7, 9, 10,
    11, 12, 13, 14, 15, 18, 33, 34, 38,
    39, 42, 44, 45, 47, 50, 56, 57, 58,
    60, 63, 64, 72, 83, 84, 91, 94, 97,
    103, 105, 108, 109, 112, 114, 118,
    120
Les Voyageurs: 1, 4, 16, 19, 21, 22,
    24, 28, 35, 41, 49, 55, 61, 62, 66,
    68, 69, 70, 71, 74, 77, 80, 81, 82,
    87, 88, 92, 93, 95, 99, 110, 111,
    113, 116, 117
The Image Bank: 3, 30, 46, 51, 76,
    85, 96, 102, 107, 123
MacQuitty International Collection:
    20, 26, 43, 53, 65, 119
ICEX, Spanish Foreign Trade
    Institute, Madrid: 5, 25, 27, 32,
    36, 89, 100